TODAY'S ROYAL MARINES

By the same author

ARK ROYAL - A PICTORIAL HISTORY
ATTACK HELICOPTERS
BATTLEFIELD HELICOPTERS
BRITISH AIRCRAFT CARRIER
BRITISH NAVAL AIR POWER
CARRIER AIR OPERATIONS
E-BOATS AND COASTAL CRAFT
ENCYCLOPAEDIA OF AVIATION
ENCYCLOPAEDIA OF THE FLEET AIR ARM SINCE 1945
ENCYCLOPAEDIA OF THE MODERN ROYAL NAVY
FLEET COMMAND
GERMAN CAPITAL SHIPS
GERMAN DESTROYERS AND ESCORTS
INVINCIBLE CLASS
JANE'S WORLD NAVAL AVIATION
MISSILE SYSTEMS
MODERN BRITISH MISSILES
MODERN MILITARY HELICOPTERS
MODERN ROYAL NAVAL WARSHIPS
NATO NAVIES OF THE 1980s
NUCLEAR-POWERED SUBMARINES
ROYAL NAVY OF THE 1980s
THE MODERN ROYAL NAVY
TODAY'S ARMY AIR CORPS
U-BOATS IN THE ATLANTIC

TODAY'S ROYAL MARINES

PAUL BEAVER

PATRICK STEPHENS

© Paul Beaver 1988

Photographs credited to the Royal Navy and Royal
Marines are British Crown Copyright.

First published in 1988

British Library Cataloguing in Publication Data

Beaver, Paul.
    Today's Royal Marines.
    1. Great Britain. *Royal Marines*
    I. Title
    359.9'6'0941   VE57

ISBN 1-85260-008-X

Front cover Commandos of the Mountain &
Arctic Warfare Cadre of the Royal Marines man
a forward observation post high in the mountains of Norway (RM).

Back cover Rigid raider of 539 Assault
Squadron RM during exercises in Norway in
support of NATO's Northern Flank (*Robin
Adshead*).

Patrick Stephens is part of the
Thorsons Publishing Group, Denington Estate,
Wellingborough, Northamptonshire, NN8 2RQ,
England

Printed in Great Britain by
B.L&U Printing Ltd., Wellingborough
Northamptonshire.

10 9 8 7 6 5 4 3 2 1

CONTENTS

FOREWORD by Major General Julian Thompson OBE
Commander of 3 Cdo Bde RM in the Falklands

One would be hard put to find so much information about the Royal Marines contained in many a book twice the size, and price, of Paul Beaver's *Today's Royal Marines*. In a handy, pocket edition, he manages to pack in a wealth of detail, from history, organization, weapons and equipment, training, and even a paragraph or two on policy. Even an old hand like myself is reminded what a versatile and yet compact organization the Corps is. If on reading the book the general reader begins to wonder if the country gets better value for its money from any other organization compared to its Royal Marines, he or she will be getting the right message.

Since the Second World War there have been several occasions when the Royal Marines' future looked decidedly shaky. There were those for an elite force of Commandos, to assault from the sea. Never again, they said, apparently gifted with the ability to foretell the future, would there be beachheads to be taken, at least not by the British. Forgetting the maxim that the enemy will have four courses of action open to him, and will choose the fifth, they were prepared to dispense with the flexibility of sea-power, in favour of measures that depended on airfields and ports being available. In other words, relying on any potential aggressor being obliging enough to fall in with our plans. Korea, Suez, Kuwait, Limbang, Tanganyika, and the Falklands proved the need to be able to project power from the sea. It is a lesson the Soviets have learned, and the build-up of their Naval Infantry is the result.

Where the Royal Marine scores, and is so cost-effective, is his ability to turn his hand to anything. Not only is he an elite infantry soldier, but possesses a range of other skills. Like all perfectionists, he makes sure that he is the best at everything he does. It is the pride in his job and determination to excel, which makes the Royal Marine the peerless commando soldier. This comes across loud and clear in *Today's Royal Marines*.

The author has rightly included a chapter on the Army units attached to Commando Forces. They are a vital part of the team. No Royal Marine, especially anyone who has seen the gunners, sappers, and other army members of the green beret family, in battle would want them to go unmentioned.

I wish Paul Beaver every success with this book, and I commend it to anyone who wants to find out about 'Today's Royal Marines'.

INTRODUCTION and ACKNOWLEDGEMENTS

It is a difficult task to prepare a book about an elite force, even as simple and straightforward an account as this, without having been one of their number. Nevertheless, the Royal Marines as a Corps supported the idea of this account which sets out to put flesh on the bones of the chapters to be devoted to the Corps in my *Encyclopaedia of the Modern Royal Navy*.

During the past five years, I have been able to take part in various Royal Marine exercises and training weekends as well as visiting barracks and other locations. To see the Arctic warfare side of the Corps operations, I spent a number of days with Zulu Company of 45 Commando Group RM in northern Norway. Other interesting and rewarding times were spent with the Hong Kong-based raiding squadron, with 845 and 846 Naval Air Squadrons in Norway, abroad HMS *Intrepid* and *Invincible* during RM embarkations, and with the Royal Marines Reserve, City of London.

I have been impressed with the professional conduct, thoroughness of the training and the ability of all those I have met. When I first began my interest in the Corps, preparing the first edition of the *Encyclopaedia*, the Corps's future was in doubt. The three qualities I have mentioned will ensure that at least the foreseeable future will be secure for Britain's sea soldiers.

I am particularly pleased to acknowledge the kindness of General Thompson in writing the foreword. In addition, my book has been supported by Captain Anthony Provest RN, the Director Public Relations (Navy) and his Royal Marines public information staff headed by Captain Rob Need RM. Four others have kindly assisted with the compilation of the book: Captain Rod Bell RM, formerly of the Commando Forces News Team; Captain Derek Oakley RM, the former editor of *Globe & Laurel*, the Corps's journal, Chief Petty Officer (Phot) Pete Holgate and Petty Officer (Phot) Alistair Campbell. Additional material was provided by Patrick Allen and Robin Walker. I would also like to acknowledge the use of various Royal Marines public relations information sheets and booklets, especially James Ladd's *Royal Marines of the 1970s and '80s* which although written prior to the Falklands conflict has confirmed many of the basic facts about the Corps.

POST-WAR HISTORY

This introduction to the elite forces of the British armed services has been written by Captain Derek Oakley MBE RM, the editor of the Corps's own journal, Globe & Laurel, *1969-86.*

The Royal Marines had seen a distinguished war between 1939 and 1945. Vast changes had been made both in thinking and action, but like any other regular force at the cessation of hostilities, it had to pick up the pieces and look forward to a peacetime role. At the outbreak of the Second World War the Corps strength had stood at 16,000 but with the influx of 'Hostilities Only' marines, it had risen to more than 75,000. Whilst the traditional sea-service role of the Corps remained, two fresh challenges had been born during these war years in Commandos and Landing Craft. By 1948 the regular strength was 13,000 Royal Marines with a small number of National Servicemen.

The peace that followed the War was completely different from

The first major post-war conflict was the Korean War where the Royal Marines served with distinction. Here two assault engineers of 41 (Independent) lay beehive charges to demolish a railway line behind enemy lines. Note the US-pattern M1 rifles (Royal Marines Museum).

that which had followed any other conflict. A 'cold war' started within months and, although it may be difficult to believe 40 years on, Great Britain was still a premier world power. Her Empire was mainly intact, she had the second largest navy in the world, and had over a million men under arms. The Socialist government, elected on 26 July 1945, pledged to reduce arms almost before the war in the Far East had ended in order to concentrate its resources on rebuilding the country. In addition its doctrine opposed the whole concept of the Empire.

The Royal Marines, as an integral part of the Royal Navy, had to take its share of the enormous reduction that peace decreed and through the ensuing three decades took its toll, being threatened more than once with complete disbandment. It took considerable courage and firm forward thinking to save the Corps from obliteration. New roles were sought in 1945 as they still are today, and it is to the credit of the Royal Marines that their strength today is related to finding, mastering and carrying out new tasks as world and particularly European demands change.

THE NEW CORPS ROLE

A parliamentary decision of October 1945 disbanded all army commandos, and thus gave the Corps an opportunity to take a role for itself which has since proved its life-blood. Only a single brigade was retained, 3rd Commando Brigade Royal Marines, then in Hong Kong as part of the occupation forces. The three Commandos assigned were 44(RM) Commando (which became 40 Cdo), 42 and 45. This retained the number of one Commando connected with each of the main theatres of the war, Italy, the Far East and North-West Europe respectively. Whilst before the War, sea-service had been the mainstay of the Corps, this new role of Commandos gave the Corps a land formation, allied to the Royal Navy, for which they were highly suited as 'sea soldiers'. Being independent, they were able to be moved easily to any area of trouble at a moment's notice. Every man in the Royal Marines was only accepted if he passed the arduous commando course, entitling him to wear the coveted green beret.

It was not long before tension in the Middle East, particularly Palestine, found the Chiefs of Staff moving the Commando Brigade to Malta. 40 Cdo took a full part in this unhappy episode of 1947/48, guarding the docks of Haifa and keeping opposing factions apart. This aspect of peace-keeping was to be a feature of most of the brush-fire incidents that the Royal Marines were involved in for the next 40 years, and this is nowhere more apparent than in Northern Ireland today. 45 Cdo joined 40 in Palestine where, not for the first or last time, they provided the final covering force before evacuation.

But it was not only Palestine that gave cause for concern. Both in Egypt and Cyprus, nationalistic forces, heartened by the success of the Israelis, also spread urban terrorism amongst the population. The three Commandos took their turns in supplying an occupation force and a steadying influence. 45 Cdo were even rushed to Aqaba in Transjordan in April 1949 when Jewish forces threatened the port.

FAR EASTERN TROUBLE SPOTS

However, it was in the Far East that terrorism in varying degrees was spreading, so in July 1949 the whole of 3 Commando Brigade embarked in the SS *Georgic* for Hong Kong, to reinforce the colony against the threat of communist aggression, which had by now reached the border of the colony with China. The Commandos' responsibility was the internal security of Victoria Island and the hundreds of small, outlying islands that make up the colony. Although they saw no action other than a few riot duties, they had a calming influence on a number of explosive incidents when refugees started to pour from the mainland into Hong Kong.

Trouble was beginning to build up in Malaya where communist terrorists, many of whom had fought alongside the British against the Japanese during the war, began to cause unrest and insurrection amongst the predominantly Malay population. The British Army was already stretched and needed support in the north of the country. In April 1950, after less than a year in Hong Kong, 3 Commando Brigade sailed for Penang and thence moved into the jungles of the northern state of Perak and part of Pahang. Individual soldiering, where a strong reliance on one's personal initiative, daring and awareness is part and parcel of a commando's make-up, was highly suited to the adaptable marine. For two-and-a-half years they patrolled deep into the jungle, developing a natural flare, matched only by the Gurkhas, for this type of soldiering.

Brigade HQ was based at Ipoh, with 40 Cdo at Kuala Kangsar, 42 at Ipoh and 45 at Tapah with a special responsibility for the holiday

Until the early 1970s, the Royal Marines were active in the Far East against Communist and other terrorist groups. This is a river patrol of 40 Commando along the River Serudong, Sabah province, Malaysia (RM).

hill station of the Cameron Highlands. Their success rate against the bandits was high, and their fitness and endurance were ideal for deep penetration patrols, which while not always contacting the enemy, ensured regular and comforting visits to the aboriginal tribes deep in the jungle on whom the terrorists relied for food and support. This was the first time that a planned 'hearts and minds' campaign was undertaken to defeat an enemy. Exhausted but still flushed with satisfaction at a job well done, 3 Commando Brigade left for the Middle East in 1952 when the situation in Malaya had improved and all but stabilized.

Meanwhile in 1950 North Korean forces backed by Communist China had invaded South Korea and a Commando was required for coastal raiding as part of the British contribution to the United Nations force. As no marines could be spared from Malaya, a fresh unit, 41 Independent Commando Royal Marines, was raised in England for the task. Flying to Japan wearing plain clothes, they were kitted out by the American forces, but still retained their green berets (and most importantly their boots!). After a number of successful coastal raids against railway tracks behind enemy lines, they were assigned to 1st US Marine Division in October 1950 and soon found themselves on the northern border of Korea in the Chosin reservoir area. Having fought their way north to help the Americans hold the line, the Chinese entered the war and their armies poured across the border. Outnumbered and in mountainous country and appalling wintry weather, the Royal Marines of 41 Cdo formed the rearguard of the American forces when they 'advanced to the sea'.

Heavy casualties were suffered and in late November the Commando was ordered to return to Japan to reform and re-equip. This they did returning to Korea to carry out more raids, some from US submarines along the coast, delaying and causing heavy casualties to the Chinese. The unit returned to UK in December 1951, finally disbanding on 22 February 1952.

RETURN TO THE MEDITERRANEAN

Royal Marines continued to serve in all the Royal Navy's major ships, battleships, cruisers and aircraft carriers, being actively involved in the Korean War, manning the guns of the fleet. The Royal Marines Band Service was completely reorganized in 1950, when the Divisional Bands, who had recruited separately, were amalgamated with musicians of the Royal Naval School of Music who had provided bands for sea, naval shore establishments and 3 Commando Brigade. Royal Marines provided the crews for many of the landing craft of the Rhine Squadron in Germany, where they remained until 1963. Meanwhile an Amphibious Warfare Squadron was raised in the Mediterranean to support 3 Commando Brigade, and most of the craft were manned by Royal Marines. They

A smart Internal Security patrol of 45 Commando in Aden during 1966 (RM Museum).

carried out numerous exercises culminating in spearheading the assault on Port Said in November 1956.

It was whilst they were having one of their quieter post-war periods that the three Commandos paraded in Malta together for a special occasion. On 29 November 1952 HRH The Prince Philip, Duke of Edinburgh carried out his first major ceremonial with the Corps when he presented each Commando with their first stand of Colours. Previously only the port divisions of Chatham, Portsmouth and Plymouth had Colours. Seven months later, on the coronation of HM The Queen, His Royal Highness was appointed Captain General of the Royal Marines.

Further cuts in personnel saw the reduction to two Commandos in the Mediterranean with a further one, 42 Cdo in embryo form at the Commando School at Bickleigh in Devon, able to be activated at a moment's notice. Indeed this reduced Commando did see some action in Northern Ireland on anti-IRA patrols in 1957, besides laying the foundation for arctic warfare when exercising in northern Norway. 40 and 45 Commandos were actively involved in the growing Cyprus emergency, moving to the troubled island in September 1955 and patrolling the Troodos mountains in search of General Grivas and his followers. There were some clashes with the dissidents, but like Malaya earlier in the decade, the contact rate was depressingly low. It took a high standard of intelligence and patrolling discipline to keep alert at all times. Many of the young men involved were National Servicemen. The Royal Marines had taken only a limited number of conscripts, and those they did absorb were of a relatively high standard. These young men quickly took on the traditions and role of their illustrious predecessors, and met up to the high standards demanded by the regulars as a personal challenge.

SUEZ LANDINGS AND THE ADEN EMERGENCY

November 1956 saw a watershed, not only in the modern history of the British armed forces, but also in British politics. Not since the Boer War, half a century before, had such a seemingly straightforward policing action brought down such wrath on Britain from other nations, particularly the United States. President Nasser of Egypt nationalized the Suez Canal only months after the British Occupation force of the Canal Zone had withdrawn. The British

Smoke hangs in the air over Port Said as helicopters and Buffalo LVTs carrying Royal Marines move in to establish a beach-head during the Suez Crisis in November 1956 (Museum of Army Flying).

government saw this as a savage blow to its pride, and along with Israel and France determined to take independent action to recover lost ground. The rest of the world saw it differently, and this was to have an adverse effect on the result. As far as the Royal Marines were concerned it was a military triumph, and was to have a lasting effect on the future of the Corps.

By September 1956 3 Commando Brigade, now reinforced by 42 Cdo from England, trained in Malta with anti-tank crews from infantry battalions, and tanks of the 6th Royal Tank Regiment. Amphibious landings were continually practised in readiness for a proposed assault on Alexandria to recover the Canal. In late October the slowest convoy since the days of Cleopatra set sail across the Mediterranean. It took six days to cover the 1,000 miles, the plans were twice changed and international pressure on the government decreed that no larger Royal Naval gun than 114 mm was to be allowed to provide supporting fire for the invasion force. At dawn on 6 November, 3 Commando Brigade assaulted the beaches of Port Said close to the entrance to the Canal in LVTs, with the following waves in LCAs. Close air support was provided by the Fleet Air Arm. The previous morning 3 Para had landed on Gamil airfield some six miles west of Port Said and taken it after some heavy fighting.

40 and 42 Cdos stormed the beaches and took their first objectives, rows of holiday villas and flats in which the occasional Egyptian soldier put up limited resistance. The beachhead now secure, 45 Cdo carried out the first ever unit helicopter landing. They lan-

ded in Whirlwind and Sycamore helicopters of the Joint Helicopter Unit and 845 Naval Air Squadron, from the aircraft carriers *Theseus* and *Ocean*. 40 Cdo moved through the commercial area and a particularly bloody fight ensued before the Canal Company's offices were taken. Meanwhile 42 Cdo, having consolidated their positions, made a dash through the town in their LVTs supported by tanks to capture the Power Station and Cold Storage Depot to the south. They met a hail of sniper fire, and Egyptian soldiers, having now discarded their uniforms, lobbed grenades from the high buildings on to the convoy.

Further objectives were defined that evening including an advance down the Canal road, but political machinations intervened. Under even more admonishment from the rest of the world, the British Government called a cease-fire at midnight and after a few uneasy weeks, with snipers still active in the town, an ignominious withdrawal of the British (and French forces who had taken Port Fuad on the east bank of the Canal) was made.

Although it had been a political disaster, the Suez operation had been a military success, but it had shown up the shortcomings of 3 Commando Brigade in its lack of supporting arms, equipment and landing craft. The slowness with which the seaborne assault was mounted threw traditional Second World War methods into disfavour. The helicopter assault clearly showed the way forward and with the firm backing of the First Sea Lord, Admiral Lord Louis Mountbatten, a new concept was born which carried the Royal Marines through the next two decades. This was the 'Commando Carrier' and the conversion of *Bulwark* was soon under way, followed two years later by *Albion*.

There was no rest for the Commando Brigade. They were soon back patrolling in the mountains of Cyprus, where their new-found helicopter techniques were given an extended outing in trying to corner guerilla groups unawares in their hides. A special 'sky cavalry' was formed between 45 Cdo and 728 Squadron's detached Flight of four Whirlwinds and they operated for six months prior to their final tour in the island which they completed in December 1958. 40 Cdo did serve one more period there in the spring of 1959.

It was in March of the following year that the Corps found new life when 42 Cdo, once more up to full strength, sailed from England in *Bulwark* for the Far East. Her hangar decks now accommodated a helicopter squadron, Land Rovers and other vehicles, assault craft and full stores to support a 600-strong Commando. After exercising in the Mediterranean, it reached Singapore in June

In the 1960s, Royal Marine Commando Air Troops formed an integral part of RM Commandos, operating the Agusta-Bell Sioux reconnaissance and liaison helicopter. This particular helicopter is photographed over the mountains of Aden in April 1965 (Royal Navy).

1960. It was not long before a Royal Marine officer joined the ship as an operational helicopter pilot, the first of many to come, which gave the Corps a renewed interest in naval aviation. The amphibious ships concept was further enhanced when two special assault ships, *Fearless* and *Intrepid*, were laid down in 1962, though they were not to see service until the end of the 1960s.

More trouble was not far away and 45 Cdo were sent from Malta to Aden in April 1960 where they became permanently based for the next seven-and-a-half years. Dissident tribesmen, reinforced from the Yemen, roamed the barren mountains and desert wastes causing unrest up country. The marines were based at Dhala in the Aden Protectorate and saw almost continual but spasmodic action in this inhospitable country. It was a one year's exhausting tour for each of them under the incessant heat where a sniper's bullet could always be expected.

SINGAPORE, KUWAIT AND THE BORNEO CONFRONTATION

The redeployment of 3 Commando Brigade to the Far East continued during 1961 with the Headquarters and 40 Cdo joining 42 Cdo in Singapore. The Corps was on a high with excellent recruiting and a strength of 10,000 as two more Commandos were reformed, 41 Cdo at Bickleigh in March 1960 followed by 43 Cdo at Plymouth in 1961. Each Commando was increased in strength to 687 officers and men and the five wartime fighting troops were reorganized into three Infantry Companies plus Support Company. It was now an all-regular Corps with the ending of National Service. It was hoped that this mobile force of the Royal Navy would be able to nip any insurrection in newly-independent Commonwealth nations in the bud. Such a role was highly fitting for the Royal Marines and continuous exercises in both the Middle and Far East with the Commando Ships were a feature of the early 1960s.

In June 1961 Iraq mobilized and threatened to take over the oil-rich state of Kuwait. *Bulwark* was exercising off Karachi with 42 Cdo embarked and they were able to be on the ground in support of the ruler of Kuwait within two days. There was no bloodshed. This was a supreme example of what a quick reaction force could achieve.

The next year found the Royal Marines in another oil-rich state, this time the British Sultanate of Brunei, on the northern coast of Borneo. A revolt broke out in early December 1962 and British hostages were taken in a number of towns. The initial force of a company of Gurkhas found the situation more than they could cope with, and 42 Cdo were quickly flown to Labuan Island and thence ferried into Brunei Town. Meanwhile 40 Cdo in *Albion* were off Mombasa and were swiftly ordered east. The task given to 42 Cdo on their arrival was to release the British Resident, his wife and several other Europeans from Limbang, 12 miles up river where the rebels were holding them.

L Company was assigned to the task, and with the help of the crews of two naval minesweepers, *Fiskerton* and *Chawton*, they commandeered two ancient Z lighters. These were quickly serviced and fortified, the company commander briefed and the small force set out at midnight on 11/12 December along the narrow river covered in mangrove swamp and barely passable in places. After laying up silently when just in sight of Limbang, the two craft, with Vickers medium machine-guns mounted in their open bows, moved off slowly at 0500. As they were approaching what appeared to be a sleeping village, the whole panorama erupted and, with heavy enemy fire being directed at them, they made a frontal assault near the police station. After an hour's fire fight, the rebels were driven off or taken prisoner and the hostages, two of whom had been threatened with execution at dawn, were released unharmed. It was a short, sharp action in which the inborn amphibious expertise of

Confrontation with Indonesia was another testing time for the Corps, much of its work being carried out far upstream. Here, a patrol moves at speed along one of the many rivers of Sarawak on Borneo island. Borneo is shared between Malaysia and Indonesia; it was the latter's claim to all the territory which led to Confrontation (via Captain Derek Oakley).

the marine was once again put to the test and not found wanting.

Although the Brunei revolt was snuffed out by this prompt action, the Russian and Indonesian trained and inspired rebels took to the jungle and for the next four years continually harassed and undermined the Sarawak and North Borneo (now Sabah) population. 3 Commando Brigade became responsible for the whole of Sarawak, an area of 50,000 square miles, nine-tenths of it covered in thick mountainous jungle. Most of the country was unmapped and the border with Indonesian Borneo was virtually indefinable. Jungle patrolling sought out the rebels, who followed the normal pattern of such groups in terrorizing local villages and demanding food and help. Like Malaya ten years before, it was only the occasional patrol which made contact with the enemy and then it was no more than a fleeting glimpse and an intense but brief fire fight before the dissidents disappeared back into the enveloping jungle. Hours of lying silently in ambushes, bitten by mosquitoes or soaked by tropical downpours, made it an uncomfortable confrontation. Once again it was the Communist influence that led to the Indonesian regular army crossing the border to pillage and sack local kampongs, quickly withdrawing behind the border shield.

Royal Marines of 40 and 42 Cdos took their turns with army battalions in this prolonged emergency. The Royal Marines Special Boats Sections carried out discreet cross-border incursions and occasionally sea and river patrols in their never-ending search for intelligence and information. Jungle craft, a high standard of training and personal initiative made the commando an ideal soldier for the job.

Back in England the Royal Marines were celebrating the tercentenary of their formation from the Trained Bands of London in 1664. HM The Queen reviewed the Corps in the grounds of Buckingham Palace, whilst a host of ceremonial and other activities marked the year. Two of these are worthy of note. Her Majesty dined with the officers of the Corps on 23 July 1964 at the Royal Naval College Greenwich. At the instigation of Admiral of the Fleet The Earl Mountbatten of Burma, then Chief of the Defence Staff, she granted the Royal Marines the privilege of drinking the Loyal Toast seated, in all their messes ashore and afloat. On the final day of tercentenary year, 27 October 1965, Lord Mountbatten was welcomed into the Corps as Life Colonel Commandant by his nephew HRH The Prince Philip, the Captain General, at an impressive parade at Eastney, Portsmouth. It was also at this time that Lovat uniform was introduced into the Corps as an alternative to 'blues' and to replace battledress.

Another small 'brush-fire' incident occurred in January 1964 when President Nyere of Tanganyika called upon British help to quell armed insurrection by his rebellious troops. *Centaur*, a conventional aircraft carrier, acted in the commando ship role by embarking 45 Commando at Aden and flying them ashore at Dar-es-Salaam by helicopters. The unit quickly established itself ashore, and with Royal Navy fighter bombers overhead, they quelled the riot in a few days with little incident. After returning to Aden, 45 Cdo immediately became involved in the Radfan campaign. This was notable for its bloody fire-fights with rebels in the rugged, bleak and mountainous regions to the north of Aden as the British prepared to withdraw from the colony. After being the last troops to leave the Radfan area, the unit became involved heavily in the infamous Crater district of Aden town, before the final withdrawal. 42 Cdo, from Singapore, joined them as a cover force for the last few days and were indeed the last to leave the colony, although that individual honour probably belongs to the Royal Marine bowman of a landing craft that evacuated the last wave on 29 November 1967. 45 Cdo returned to England and Stonehouse Barracks, Plymouth.

WITHDRAWAL FROM THE EMPIRE

It was at this time that retrenchment and further cutbacks were being imposed on all the armed forces, the Royal Navy suffering worst of all. Their world–wide role was diminishing as British possessions in the east were being handed over to independent rule. As their numbers decreased, so too did those of the Corps, traditionally 10 per cent of the Navy's vote. 43 Cdo was disbanded in 1968, and 3 Commando Brigade had all returned to the UK by 1972. The Corps sought a new role, and with their commitment to the northern and southern flanks of NATO, they found a fresh and exciting future. The arctic wastes of northern Norway were a far cry from the jungles of Malaya and Borneo. 45 Cdo, based on Arbroath, became the arctic warfare specialists and every man was taught military skiing and survival in the snow. The Royal Netherlands Marine Corps provided 'Whiskey' Company in 1973 to serve and operate with 45 and wear their red unit lanyard, denoting membership of 'Four Five'.

Meanwhile 41 Cdo, who had been the first Royal Marines unit to serve in Northern Ireland during a 'Spearhead' duty in 1969, found themselves in sunnier climes when they were sent as garrison troops to Malta in September 1971. During their eight years on the island, they exercised as far afield as Turkey, Sardinia and even Puerto Rico. They carried out a tour in Cyprus with the United Nations forces in 1974/75. The unit was reduced to Company strength in 1977 and finally withdrawn altogether in March 1979. 41 Cdo suffered a temporary disbandment, then a brief resurgence before once again falling to the government's axe in 1981. However, it was not before they had had the honour of representing the Royal Marines on Public Duties in London in November 1978, the first time the Corps had performed these Royal duties since 1935.

Royal Marines detachments had also been reduced at sea, along with the size of the modern fleet. Apart from the three commando and assault ships where marines manned the landing craft, detachments were now confined to frigates and the ice patrol vessel *Protector*. Sergeants were now the senior ranks at sea in most cases. They saw some excitement during the Atlantic 'Cod War' and there was a small garrison, Naval Party 8901 in the Falkland Islands. Here they were involved in an incident in 1966 when a group of Argentine 'nationalists' hijacked an airliner and landed at Port Stanley intent on capturing the islands. The Royal Marines surrounded the plane and the incident passed off quietly.

In March 1976, Salerno Flight of 41 Commando Group, Royal Marines, based at St Georges in Malta undertook pilot navigation training in mountain flying in nearby Sicily (Capt Rodney Helme RM).

Nearer home 45 Cdo had set up a base at Elvegardsmoen in north Norway in January 1970 and the first 242 marines savoured the delights of an arctic winter training the following year. From these humble beginnings the Mountain and Arctic Warfare Cadre was established and they are now the acknowledged experts at their winter warfare trade. There has been no improvement in the Northern Ireland situation and Commandos have taken their turn with army units in four month roulement deployments, completing 24 such tours by 1987. In 1979 40 Cdo spent a year in Londonderry, and were not far away when the Life Colonel Commandant, Earl Mountbatten of Burma, was brutally assassinated whilst holidaying with his family in Mullaghmore. At his funeral the Royal Marines played a prominent part, one band immediately preceding the cortège in the procession, whilst a Royal Marines funeral firing party paid its last respects at Romsey Abbey.

Although the Commandos were based in Britain, this did not stop them from answering emergency calls abroad. One such came to 42 Cdo in September 1979 when they were despatched to Hong Kong where the influx of illegal immigrants from the mainland into the colony became a flood. Their amphibious prowess, especially with small speedy raiding craft was used to the full in the tortuous waterways that make up the New Territories of Hong Kong. Although the Commando only stayed for two months, a permanent Royal Marines Raiding Squadron was set up and is still in the colony on operational patrols. It is a measure of the Corps's readiness to meet any contingency that, in the autumn of 1979, all three Commandos were operationally deployed, 40 Cdo being in Cyprus, 42 in Hong Kong and 45 in Northern Ireland.

Little did 42 Cdo expect to be in the Far East again within 12 months. This time it was to the New Hebrides, a condominium with France, where unrest broke out just prior to the islands being declared the independent state of Vanuatu. A tactical HQ and an enlarged Company Group were flown there, restored the authority of the government and took park in the ceremonial side of the independence celebrations.

CALL TO THE SOUTH ATLANTIC

Naval Party 8901 had continued to garrison the Falkland Islands with Royal Marines providing the 40 strong detachment. It was held in such esteem by the locals that the Corps was granted the Freedom of Stanley in December 1976, a singular honour. This 'lost' garrison suddenly hit the headlines when the Argentinians, trying to rid their minds from the economic chaos that riddled their own country, invaded the islands on 2 April 1982. Previously they had landed a small party at a whaling station in South Georgia. In Stanley, the Royal Marines rallied to the Governor's call and put up spirited resistance. It was soon apparent that this small detachment was hopelessly outnumbered and the governor ordered them to surrender. On the following day more Argentinians invaded South Georgia, where the Royal Marines from *Endurance* had set up a defensive position. For two-and-a-half hours the Royal Marines fought off the invaders, even scoring a direct hit on a corvette with a hand-held anti-tank rocket launcher. But superior numbers forced them to surrender to avoid further casualties.

In Britain, the government was shocked into urgent action and the Royal Marines were the first to answer the call. 3 Commando Brigade was placed at 72 hours, notice to sail, and although marines were on leave as far away as the USA, Tunisia and Zimbabwe, the three units were fully mobilized and ready to move within 48 hours. The main naval Task Force sailed from Portsmouth on 5 April, while many merchant ships, including SS *Canberra*, RMS *Queen Elizabeth II* and a number of roll-on roll-off ferries were taken up from trade. *Canberra* sailed on 9 April with 40 and 42 Cdos embarked along with 3 Para, who had been placed under command. It was a remarkable achievement, proving once again the instant readiness of the

The light aircraft carrier HMS Hermes was the last British LPH (Landing Platform Helicopter), pictured here on her final deployment to the Mediterranean Sea in 1983 — but not before she had been the command ship for Operation Corporate, the liberation of the Falkland Islands.

Services to react to any emergency, even one 8,000 miles away.

A short stop was made at Ascension Island, where the troops were able to shake themselves out, stretch their legs and test fire their weapons. Vehicles and stores were cross-decked between ships to make a realistic landing pattern, and the Brigade Headquarters worked overtime to formulate a plan for the recovery of the islands. Knowing that the enemy would outnumber the invaders, the Royal Marines planners banked on surprise, a higher standard of military fitness and superior training to outmatch the Argentinians. The solution was not one that would endear it to the pundits at the military Staff Colleges. Political pressure was brought to bear on the commanders through the ease of modern communications, and an unprecedented press corps accompanied the Task Force extracting every scrap of information for release to the expectant public in Britain. Never before had families lived so close to a war that their loved ones were fighting on the other side of the world.

Rigorous physical training took place on board each ship as the Task Force steamed south into the inhospitable wastes of the southern Atlantic. As they approached the Falklands, Argentine air attacks with Exocet missiles took their toll, but luckily, none of the troop carriers was hit. Teams from Royal Marines Special Boats Sections and Special Air Service patrols had already been landed on the Falklands to seek out intelligence on enemy strengths and dispositions. Those in the main force were cheered by the news that a Company Group from 42 Cdo had recaptured South Georgia on

The liberation of South Georgia involved both the Special Boat Squadron and the Special Air Service Regiment in Special Forces' operations. Here a member of the SF team passes a missile-armed Westland Wasp helicopter aboard HMS Plymouth.

24 April after a brief action in which an Argentinian submarine was sunk.

At dawn on 21 May 3 Commando Brigade stormed ashore at Port San Carlos, some fifty miles from Stanley, in landing craft manned entirely by Royal Marines. Overhead, along with the troop-carrying helicopters of the Royal Navy, were Royal Marines pilots in light helicopters. The only casualties in the landings were when two of these helicopters were shot down. Within 24 hours the whole Brigade of four units was ashore, with 2 Para leading the way. Logistic resources were stretched to the limit, but political pressure from London urged those on the ground 'to get on with it'. The successful but costly attack on Goose Green and Darwin by 2 Para was the start. Lack of helicopters and transport led 45 Cdo and 3 Para, with loads often exceeding 110 lbs, to the great 'yomp' across 50 miles of ferocious, rugged country in freezing temperatures and continual rain to the heights overlooking the capital of Stanley, where it was known the Argentinians would make their main stand.

The arrival of Major General Jeremy Moore, a Royal Marine who had won Military Crosses in Malaya and Borneo, as Commander of the Land Forces along with 5 Infantry Brigade, allowed Brigadier Julian Thompson to concentrate on the task of defeating the enemy's last defence line. A bold night attack was planned with two Commandos and a Parachute Battalion carrying out simultaneous attacks on prominent features. It was known that the enemy was

The terrain in the Falkland Islands was not unlike the traditional Royal Marines' training ground on Dartmoor, but the weather was described as 'twice as bad'. These are marines from K Company, 42 Commando RM, advancing towards Mount Challenger (Cdo Forces News Team/CPO Holdgate).

well dug in, but it was thought that their morale was low. The attacks were made on the night of 11/12 June, some of them through enemy minefields, all relying on daring flanking movements up rocky hills and crags. Heavy covering fire was provided from the Royal Artillery's Commando Light Regiment and guns from HM ships. The attack was entirely successful, starting with a silent approach and culminating in hand-to-hand fighting against some determined resistance. By dawn it was clear that the end was near, though 2nd Battalian Scots Guards did have a tough fight for Tumbledown Mountain and 2 Para for Wireless Ridge.

General Moore took the Argentinian surrender at 2100 hours on 14 June. The Royal Marines had added another laurel to add to the globe on their cap badge. Over half the Corps was involved in the South Atlantic, and the price they paid was 27 killed and over 100 wounded. However, despite the euphoria of their welcome home, defence cuts continued and there is still a question over replacement amphibious shipping for them to carry out their NATO role effectively.

Reflecting the inner-looking response today is the Royal Marines' increasing role in naval security. The need to protect Britain's off-shore oil rigs against sabotage and an increasing awareness of the potential Soviet threat of terrorist attacks has given the Corps yet another new role. Comacchio Group based in Scotland was specially formed for this task. In keeping with their 'out-of-area' role, 40 Cdo spent six months as the resident 'battalion' in Belize while Commandos still regularly take their turn with the army in Northern Ireland.

For the third time in their history the Corps was invited to perform London Public Duties in 1986, a task which fell to 42 Cdo when they paraded with the new SA 80 weapon for the first time. Thus the Royal Marines continue, their excellence both in action and on parade unsurpassed. They have survived many crises in the past and have come through them all relatively unscathed. No doubt this highly-trained and dedicated Corps will emerge even stronger in the future. They are always seeking and mastering new roles to keep them as the spearhead of Britain's armed forces. 'Per Mare Per Terram' (By sea, by land) is their motto, and it is to be hoped that they will continue to be Britain's Sea Soldiers for many years to come.

TODAY'S ROLE

It has been said many times before, but the Royal Marines are the Royal Navy's military force — the British sea soldiers. A small but powerful force, the Corps has both a national defence role and one assigned to NATO. Their versatility includes the protection of oil rig facilities, protecting important bases, counter-terrorism, reconnaissance behind enemy lines and amphibious warfare.

COMMANDO FORCES

The landing force element of the United Kingdom Amphibious Force, which is declared to the North Atlantic Treaty Organization (NATO) and which would be assigned to the Supreme Allied Commander Atlantic (SACLANT) in time of war, is the primary task of the field force element of the Royal Marines. It is envisaged that the assignment would be to Northern European Command (NEC) which encompasses Norway, Denmark and North Germany. This reinforcement operation is designed to deny the area of the enemy and to prevent his interference with the transatlantic resupply routes in time of war or tension.

The field force of the Royal Marines goes by the title of Commando Forces and they continue to have an important role to play in NATO strategy for the prevention of conflict but in addition for the defence of Europe in that event.

It is not possible for Cdo Forces to acquire all the necessary expertise that is required from within the Corps, so there are elements of the Royal Navy and of the British Army integrated into the order of battle. Nevertheless, many of those from other services are expected to undergo the rigorous All Arms Commando Course at the Commando Training Centre, Lympstone. It is only when they have passed this course that they are entitled to wear the coveted green beret and work alongside the Royal Marines.

MOUNTAIN AND ARCTIC WARFARE

As one of the major defence obligations of the Royal Navy is to supply, sustain and support the British element of the joint UK/Netherlands amphibious force, it is not surprising that there is a

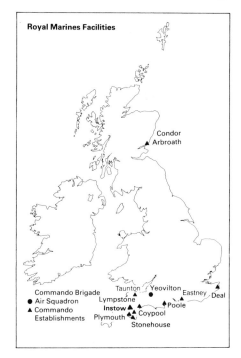

close working relationship between the Royal Marines and their Dutch counterparts.

The first exercises in this role were carried out in 1970 and since then the Corps has shown its abilities in the Arctic winter every year since. Specialist vehicles and other equipment have been acquired for this role, including the use of Swedish-built oversnow tractors, starting with the Snotrac in 1971 and progressing through the Volvo Bv202E by 1980, leading to the deployment of a further requirement for the late 1980s.

AMPHIBIOUS ROLE

Since the early 1960s, a modern amphibious role for the Royal Marines has been considered important to the defence of the United Kingdom and its interests overseas. The exact level of that importance has, however, been open to frequent argument and debate, although the success of the landing operations – Operation Sutton – during the Falklands campaign seems to have forestalled current plans of disbandment.

A ski patrol sets out from a Norwegian beach-head. In the 1970s and 1980s, mountain and arctic warfare has become the forte of the Royal Marine Commando forces, with a NATO role of defending the Northern Flank area in Norway.

In recent years, the general premise has been that the Royal Marines has an acknowledged and vital role to support the extreme flanks of Norway and Turkey in the event of tension and/or war with the Soviet Union and her allies in the Warsaw Pact. In addition, there are the 'out of (NATO) area' operations typified by the Falklands and the Armilla Patrol where the Corps's talents can be well used.

Assault ships, like HMS Intrepid *seen here entering Portsmouth, are now the primary means of transporting Royal Marine Commandos. Doubt still remains over their future even after their highly successful operations in the Falklands* (Robin Walker).

The Northern Flank reinforcement supports the generally-held view that Commando Forces would be transported and if necessary landed to support Norwegian and other NATO forces protecting the northern flank at a time of tension rather than assaulting a beach-head. Present NATO doctrine does not favour invasion in the US forces Grenada style, especially because of the risks (proven in Grenada) of such operations. Although the reinforcement of the Northern Flank is now a NATO commitment, the critics of the amphibious role for the Royal Marines have said that the assault ships and logistical support ships could not 'live' in the Norwegian Sea in war because the weapons environment would be too hostile. Others would like to see costs cut by landing troops in time of tension by ro-ro ferry or other ships taken up from trade (STUFT) rather than amphibious assault ships (LPD) like *Fearless* and *Intrepid*.

The Southern Flank scenario is similar to that for Norway but is based upon aggression against Greece or Turkey from outside the membership of the North Atlantic Alliance. Regular exercises are carried out by British and allied forces under the designation Exercise Display Determination which aims to improve inter-operability between member nations tasked with the security of the Eastern Mediterranean.

In 1986 the UK Government decided to review the update of the Landing Platform Dock (LPD) replacement by asking for industry proposals of a refurbishment of the existing hulls, a new naval-manned design or the use of Royal Fleet Auxiliary Service (civilian) manned ships to be known as Aviation Support Ships (ASS). The ASS would be capable of landing 800 men by the use of helicopters and landing craft, including the provision to put at least one company ashore in the first wave. The ships would also have their own self-defence systems. A decision was not due until mid-1988 but in the meantime there were a number of unsolicited proposals from British Aerospace, British Shipbuilders, Harland & Wolff, Swan Hunter and Vickers Shipbuilding and Engineering.

What the critics have not fully considered is the limited war situation where a hostile power, usually considered by western military planners to be the Soviet Union, invades one or more of the Atlantic Islands — Iceland, Shetland, the Faroes, etc — to put pressure on the Alliance which would not risk all-out nuclear or Central Front conventional conflict by over-responding to the invasion. In that case – another Falklands – the Royal Marines

Future Royal Marine operations could be mounted from Aviation Support Ships like mv Contender Argent, seen here in this British Aerospace artist's impression. Naval architects Hart Fenton & Co have designed a conversion from the merchant ship design which would allow a full Commando of 803 men to embark with stores and vehicles.

would be the primary force used to defend the interests of the Alliance and country invaded.

The amphibious capability was demonstrated in 1982 with the liberation of the Falkland Islands. Although that particular type of conflict will probably not be fought again, it is not possible to predict where British interests will be directly threatened in a limited war situation. Only months before the Argentine invasion the idea of going to war with that country was remote enough for, reportedly, the Ministry of Defence to scale down intelligence gathering in that part of the world and to declare the only regular British warship –*Endurance* – surplus to requirements.

Historically, the Commando Carriers (LPHs), converted Light Fleet aircraft carriers were used in this role, but successive Labour administrations who apparently saw them as 'imperialistic' tools brought about their demise. The last, *Hermes*, was decommissioned in 1983 to sell to India as a Harrier-carrier, ironically by a Conservative government.

The ASS mentioned above could be classed as a replacement for the Landing Platform Helicopter (LPH), an asset which has been missed by both Royal Marines and Royal Navy since 1983. Aviation

HMS Hermes *offshore amongst the Norwegian fjords with both Royal Marines support* *helicopters and Sea Harrier fighters embarked. Note the LCVPs hanging down from the* *davits amidships.*

support has been lacking since *Hermes* was paid off, because the LPDs are not large enough for major helicopter operations.

Since then the Royal Navy has occasionally provided an 'Invincible' Class CVS for the LPH role, but it is highly unlikely that one would be available in either tension or war. They undoubtedly will be used for anti-submarine warfare duties to defend NATO reinforcement convoys coming across the Atlantic from North America.

THE ASSAULT SHIPS

The future of the two assault ships in the Royal Navy, *Fearless*, and *Intrepid*, was called into question in the 1981 Defence Review, but as a result of the successful amphibious operation at San Carlos under Operation Corporate, the UK Government has reconsidered their future.

According to the 1987 Defence Review, the defence of the NATO Northern Region 'is of crucial importance to the United Kingdom'. To assist with the deployment of Commando Forces to the northern Flank and to retain an amphibious capability in the longer term, the life of *Fearless* and *Intrepid* had been extended until the mid-1990s.

RFA Sir Lancelot demonstrates its ability to carry a mexiflote amidships prior to a landing operation, during Exercise Purple Warrior in November 1987, the largest post-war amphibious exercise to date. Note in the foreground a multiple Shorts Blowpipe launcher on the flight deck of a 'Rover' class Light Fleet Tanker.

In addition, six Landing Ships Logistic (LSL) will be maintained and the replacement *Sir Galahad* for the LSL sunk after the raid on Bluff Cove in 1982 entered service in December 1987. These vessels are merchant ships which belong to the Ministry of Defence and are manned by the Royal Fleet Auxiliary Service.

Each LSL is capable of carrying 340 tons of cargo right up on to a beach and unloading it through the forward clam-shell doors and ramp. Alternatively, it is possible to use the stern ramp and load vehicles and equipment on to mexiflotes or landing craft. The ships are equipped with a flight deck right aft and a landing area amidships from where netted loads for helicopters from the Royal Air Force's Boeing Chinook HC 1 to the Royal Marines' Gazelle AH 1 are prepared.

In transit the LSLs can carry three Gazelles, two Lynx AH 1, two Sea King HC 4 or three Wessex HU 5 helicopters. The helicopters can also be used to carry ashore the 402 troops which can be carried for short to medium sea crossings.

Following the Falklands conflict, the damaged *Sir Tristram* was towed back to the United Kingdom and refitted by Tyne Ship-repairers; work included lengthening the hull by 8.9 m, and the remaining four in the class will have this refit in future.

The new *Sir Galahad* has several important improvements which

The new RFA Sir Galahad was handed over to the Royal Fleet Auxiliary on 25 November 1987 and represents an important improvement in the logistical life of amphibious forces and for conventional reinforcement. Many lessons learned from the tragedy at Bluff Cove were built into the new ship (Swan Hunter).

will ease the lot of the Commando Forces it will support. Although only 339 troops are carried, the new ship has increased endurance, a longer bow ramp, higher operating speed and better air defence systems. In fact some 20 years of experience has been built into the *Sir Galahad* design, including the ability to take the medium-lift Chinook amidships and the Sea King aft, operating simultaneously. Both helicopter 'spots' have refuelling points.

OUT OF AREA

In April 1982, Argentine forces invaded the Falkland Islands in the South Atlantic and the British response showed just how important the Royal Marines are in an Out of (NATO) Area operation. Operation Corporate, the liberation of the Islands, is said to have ensured the future of the Corps which was under threat from the financial cuts proposed in the 1981 Defence Review.

Royal Marines train for various non-European terrain operations, including the undertaking of jungle warfare courses in Belize (Central America) and Brunei (Far East). It is envisaged that such a role would include the protection of British interests abroad, the evacuation of British citizens from a foreign trouble spot and supporting of national interests.

HOME DEFENCE

Naval shore establishments detachments guard a number of key establishments whose installations require safeguarding by tough troops with special skills to defeat specialist enemy units and saboteurs. Special detachments have been formed for this purpose and the commentator must presume that establishments which require special guard will include NATO and national headquarters, as well as naval facilities such as the nuclear submarine base complexes. The very nature of this kind of operation means that no further details are available from official sources.

THE ROYAL MARINES AND NORTHERN IRELAND

Since the resurgence of terrorist trouble in 1969, the Royal Marines have been deployed to the Province of Northern Ireland in rotation with British Army units on four-month emergency tours. The first such tour was in September 1969 when 41 Commando (disbanded in May 1981) was deployed to the Divis Street area of Belfast and it was followed by 45 Cdo taking on the first four-month tour in 1970 and 40 Cdo undertook the first one-year tour in 1979.

Left A troop from 45 Cdo during peacekeeping operations in Northern Ireland where the Royal Marines have undertaken their share of deployments as infantry battalions supporting the civil power (Royal Marines).

Right Ceremonial is still an important part of the Royal Marines. This is the band of Commander-in-Chief Naval Home Command on parade in front of HMS Victory in Portsmouth Dockyard (RM).

During the last two decades, the Royal Marines have also carried out duties as Resident Battalion in Londonderry and South Armagh. Internal Security (IS) operations were not a major part of the RM training programme although men embarked with ships' detachments are expected to form a landing party for such operations but on a much more limited scale than in Northern Ireland. Crowd control, riot prevention, anti-sniper patrolling and general surveillance duties, in support of the Royal Ulster Constabulary, have been improved as a result of practical experience and taking advice from other army and police units.

All commandos are given a period of intensive training prior to a posting to the Province and the unit operates purely as an infantry unit without support weapons. Peace keeping and IS do not require Milan anti-tank missiles and mortars. Regular patrols are co-ordinated from observation posts and teams are often led by NCOs.

CEREMONIAL

The Royal Marines Band Service is described elsewhere in this book (page 77) and although it does not have a fully-fledged defence role, the Service does play an important part in the role of the

Corps. Not only are the bandsmen employed in medical, first aid and other support duties in time of conflict, but they also contribute to the peacetime role.

Royal Marines ceremonial is a vital part of the tradition and heritage of the Royal Marines and it is unthinkable to consider the Senior Service without such a role. The 1987 decision to retain the Royal Marines School of Music at Deal and not to amalgamate service music has been applauded in every quarter for that reason.

Ceremonial duties include parades and guarding members of the Royal Family. Beating Retreat remains a performance at which the Band of the Royal Marines with the Corps of Drums excels.

In addition, the Royal Marines provide a nautical element to lough and sea patrols. Sea-going intelligence officers with the regular naval patrols are often marines whose primary duty is to assist in the prevention of arms smuggling and terrorism in coastal and inshore waters. During the famous Operation Motorman clearance of so-called 'no-go' areas in 1972, bulldozing equipment was brought in with the aid of landing craft from the Assault Ship *Fearless*.

ORGANIZATION AND COMMAND

The Royal Marines have a long tradition of being the Royal Navy's sea soldiers and the relationship between the Corps, the Royal Navy and other services has grown closer during the post war period. The Royal Marines, although basically organized along army lines, is controlled by the Admiralty Board of the Royal Navy through the Commandant General Royal Marines (CGRM) and his department in the Ministry of Defence.

Right *Commandant General of the Royal Marines is Lieutenant General Sir Martin Garrod KCB OBE, a former commanding officer of 40 Commando and Commander of 3 Commando Brigade Royal Marines. He is pictured here in his Ceremonial Blue Uniform (RM).*

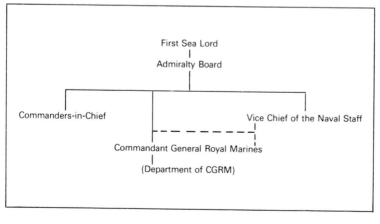

```
                    First Sea Lord
                          |
                   Admiralty Board
                          |
        ┌─────────────────┼─────────────────────┐
 Commanders-in-Chief      |        Vice Chief of the Naval Staff
                          ┌┴ ─ ─ ─ ─ ─ ─ ─ ┐
              Commandant General Royal Marines
                          |
                 (Department of CGRM)
```

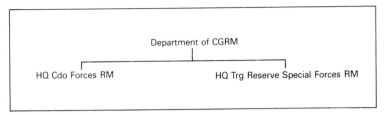

Within the Corps itself, there are two principle elements which go to make up the Royal Marines in the 1980s: HQ Commando Forces RM (HQ Cdo Forces RM) and HQ Training, and Special Reserve Forces RM. The CGRM is a Lieutenant General and his two subordinate commanders are Major General rank, as is his Chief of Staff.

HQ COMMANDO FORCES RM

The Major General Commando Forces has his headquarters at Mount Wise, Stonehouse, Plymouth, from where he is the administrative head of the fighting arm which includes 3rd Commando Brigade Royal Marines (3 Cdo Bde RM) based at Stonehouse Barracks, Plymouth, the Commando units, the specialist units, the attached units from the British Army, RM Condor Base and the Garrison Company at Plymouth.

Under current organization, HQ 3 Cdo Bde RM has operational command of all the field force units in the United Kingdom but

As part of NATO's policy of inter-member co-operation, the Royal Marines and the Royal Netherlands Marine Corps train and exercise together. Whiskey Company, RNLMC, is an integral part of 45 Commando Group, with a war role in Norway (Commando Forces News Team/CPO Holdgate).

when the brigade moves overseas, for example to Norway, MGRM Cdo Forces assumes operational command of the field force units remaining in the UK.

Besides the British units in the field force, HQ 3 Cdo Bde has operational control, from time to time, of Whiskey Company and 1 Amphibious Command Group of the Royal Netherlands Marine Corps. The Dutch marines are normally based at Doorn.

For amphibious and certain other reinforcement operations, the Fleet Air Arm provides two front line Naval Air Commando squadrons (with RN and RM aircrew) to supplement the 3 Cdo Bde Air Squadron and to provide troop and material lift and logistical support. When this happens, operational control can be assumed by HQ 3 Cdo Bde RM.

3RD COMMANDO BRIGADE

With a headquarters at Plymouth, this command of about 3,000 men provides the basic administration, command and control for the field force of the Royal Marines. From time to time, units in 3 Cdo Bde RM will take their turn with battalions of the regular army

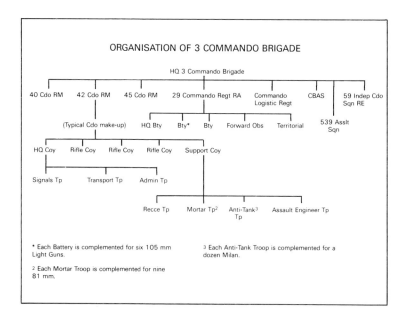

ORGANISATION OF 3 COMMANDO BRIGADE

HQ 3 Commando Brigade

40 Cdo RM | 42 Cdo RM | 45 Cdo RM | 29 Commando Regt RA | Commando Logistic Regt | CBAS | 59 Indep Cdo Sqn RE

(Typical Cdo make-up) | HQ Bty | Bty* | Bty | Forward Obs | Territorial | 539 Asslt Sqn

HQ Coy | Rifle Coy | Rifle Coy | Rifle Coy | Support Coy

Signals Tp | Transport Tp | Admin Tp

Recce Tp | Mortar Tp[2] | Anti-Tank[3] Tp | Assault Engineer Tp

* Each Battery is complemented for six 105 mm Light Guns.

[3] Each Anti-Tank Troop is complemented for a dozen Milan.

[2] Each Mortar Troop is complemented for nine 81 mm.

Somewhere in the snows of Norway, the mobile command headquarters of 3 Cdo Bde RM has been erected overnight and is fully functional within two hours. A second command post is then set up ready for a move as the battle moves or as events dictate.

to form the Spearhead Battalion which is a quick reaction force ready to move at short notice to anywhere in the world. Operations undertaken by Commando units include Northern Ireland reinforcement (1972 and 1977), Cyprus Emergency (1974) and the New Hebrides (1980) and the South Atlantic (1982).

An integral part of 3 Cdo Bde are the three Commando units (see page 51 for details), the specialist units (page 56) and the attached units of artillery and engineers (page 79). Directly supporting the brigadier is his HQ and Signal Squadron (page 45).

UNIT ORGANIZATION

Although basically using the British Army formation organization, the Royal Marines has some distinct features which have resulted from the Corps's unusual roles and specialist operations.

Commando This is the basic organization unit of 3 Cdo Bde RM. There are three Commandos currently in being, including 45 Cdo Group which has support units permanently attached. A Commando is commanded by a Lieutenant Colonel and corresponds to a battalion in British Army terms.

HQ Company This is the administrative and 'regimental' organization within a Commando and it is commanded by a senior Captain or Major.

SUBORDINATE UNITS

Motor Transport Troop This provides the Commando with its fighting and support vehicles, including Land Rovers and Volvo BV 202s. It is commanded by a Lieutenant.

Signals Troop Provides all radio and other electronic communications for the Commando, commanded by a Lieutenant.

Admin Elements Keep the paperwork up to date; provide through the Quartermaster (QM) all logistic support, and cater for all the Commando's medical, educational and administrative needs.

Rifle Company Three of these make up the fighting units of a Commando and they are commanded by a Captain RM. The full strength complement is a further five officers and 120 marines.

SUBORDINATE UNITS

Rifle Troop There are three of these in every Rifle Company, commanded by a Second Lieutenant or Lieutenant with 35 marines. A Sergeant is usually second-in-command.

Section Each Rifle Troop is made up of three sections, each with a Corporal in command, a Lance Corporal who is generally second-in-command, and there are seven other marines.

Support Company This unit is often commanded by a senior captain, but more generally a major. It provides specialist support equipment, such as mortars and anti-tank protection, assault engineers and reconnaissance.

SUBORDINATE UNITS

Recce Troop Carries out all reconnaissance and 'behind the lines' operations, using various specialist modes of transport.

Mortar Troop Complemented for nine 81 mm mortars.

Anti-Tank Troop Using the Milan anti-tank missile system to sup-

Part of a rifle troop dig in and make a firing pit for the 7.62 mm General Purpose Machine-Gun. Note that the marines are wearing NBC clothing and Green Berets.

An anti-tank troop of 42 Commando digs in with the Euromissile Milan anti-armour guided weapon during an exercise on Salisbury Plain.

port Commando operations, now supplemented by the Lynx/ TOW helicopters and capable of being transported into front line positions by air. Twelve Milan firing posts are held by the Troop.

Assault Engineer Troop Used for mine clearance and other specialist engineering feats.

Air Defence Troop is subordinate to Headquarters 3 Commando Brigade and is armed with the Javelin shoulder-launched anti-aircraft missile.

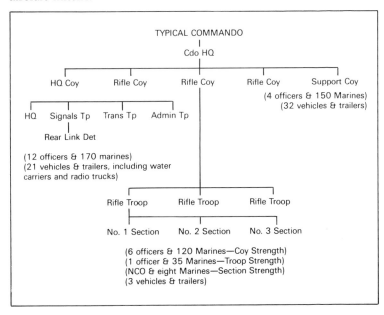

A command post set up in Norway. Note the small signs adjacent to each Bv 202 truck and its add-on tenting in which the various functions of the Brigade or Commando are carried out.

HEADQUARTERS AND SIGNALS SQUADRON

When the role of the Commando Forces was revised in the early 1970s, some of the smaller units were amalgamated into a more coherent and therefore more operationally efficient unit. Amongst the units involved was HQ and Camp 3 Cdo Bde and Signals Squadron RM and the new unit was named 3 Commando Brigade HQ and Signals Squadron Royal Marines, based at Stonehouse Barracks, Plymouth.

The Squadron's role is simply to provide the environment and facilities to enable the Brigade Commander and his Staff to control 3 Cdo Bde RM in time of peace, tension or war. In this modern age of communications and a perceived radio jamming environment, it is an important role.

Commanded by a Major RM, the unit is broken down into specialist troops plus 1 Raiding Squadron RM (see page 49):

Command Troop contains the senior staff, officers and other HQ personnel, as well as the Defence Section to protect the Command Post(s) on land. Landing Zone Marshalling Teams are also included in this Troop.

Administrative Troop, commanded by the Quartermaster, looks after the basic needs of the Squadron.

Communications Troop, commanded by a Lieutenant RM, provides all radio facilities for the Headquarters and carries out second line communications equipment repair.

Motor Transport Troop provides the vehicles for land operations, including the more conventional wheeled vehicles like Land Rovers and the oversnow tracked Volvos. It is the largest Troop in the Brigade and commanded by a Lieutenant RM.

Royal Marines Police Troop is responsible for law and order within the whole of Commando Forces and is commanded by a police-trained Lieutenant RM.

Air Defence Troop, commanded by a Lieutenant RM is armed with Shorts Blowpipe (being replaced by Javelin) shoulder-launched surface-to-air guided missiles for point defence.

Tactical Air Control Party is made up of three sections (605, 611 and 612), each commanded by a Lieutenant RM and affiliated to a Commando to provide that unit with specialist forward air control for strikes by close air support aircraft and anti-tank helicopters within the Brigade's tactical area of operations.

HQ TRAINING, RESERVE AND SPECIAL FORCES

Based at Eastney Barracks (Portsmouth, Hampshire), the headquarters of the Major General Training, Reserve and Special Forces includes a number of establishments. Under this command come the amphibious warfare base at Poole (Dorset), the Commando Training Centre at Lympstone (Devon), Comacchio Group (Arbroath, Scotland), the barracks at Eastney, the Royal Marines School of Music at Deal (Kent), the Amphibious Trials & Training Unit RM at Instow (Devon) and the various Royal Marines Reserve units.

Royal Marines Poole is the headquarters of the amphibious, landing craft, beach assault, ships' detachment and special boat squadron. The base is located on the shore at Poole and provides a training venue for much of the swimmer-canoeist special qualifications courses.

Commando Training Centre Royal Marines (CTCRM) at Lympstone is ideally suited for commando training with a close proximity to the moorland of Devon and Cornwall. Officer and marine recruits train together here in addition to many of the specialist, command and upgrading courses.

Amphibious Trials & Training Unit Royal Marines

Amphibious trials with landing craft (background) and raiding craft (slung from the forklift for ease of movement) are carried out at various locations, such as Lee-on Solent, shown here, under the auspices of Amphibious Trials and Training Unit at Instow, Cornwall.

(ATTURM) at Instow is responsible for research, development and trials into the technical side of amphibious operations. Trials have recently included the waterproofing of RM vehicles, associated equipment and systems, as well as pioneering beach recovery and assault engineering work. The new LCVP Mk 4 was trialled here immediately after the Falklands conflict.

ROYAL MARINES RESERVE

The Royal Marines Reserve (RMR) is a commando-trained volunteer force which in time of war or tension – or 'mobilization' – is ready and able to join the Regular Corps, either as specialist sub-units or as individual reinforcements.

Under the terms of the Royal Marines Act 1947, two units of reserve Royal Marines were formed at Glasgow and London under the aegis of the Royal Marine Forces Volunteer Reserve (RMFVR). In 1963, the RMR was formed from the sure foundations of the RMFVR, which title has lost some of its message with the disbandment of National Service.

Today there are five units and ten detachments with some 70 officers and 1,100 other ranks. The units and detachments are:

RMR City of London; Portsmouth Detachment; Chatham Detachment.

RMR Scotland; Dundee Detachment; Greenock Detachment; Arbroath Detachment.

RMR Bristol; Cardiff Detachment; Poole Detachment,

Raised in a number of locations around the United Kingdom, the Royal Marines Reserve is an important part of the reinforcement plans of the Corps in wartime. These are marines from the City of London unit training on Salisbury Plain.

Lympstone Detachment; Plymouth Detachment.
RMR Merseyside; Liverpool Detachment.
RMR Tyne; no Detachments.

The RMR has a good, close relationship with neighbouring RNR units and the Territorial Army. In several cases the RMR shares common establishments with the RNR. In addition, the RNR has always provided medical assistance and back-up for the RMR and several Reserve Medical Assistants have worn the coveted green beret and the right to wear the exclusive 'Royal Navy Commando (R)' shoulder flash.

Recruiting is from all walks of life from chartered surveyor to butcher, but the applicant must be physically fit and mentally alert. He must also be dedicated to his part-time vocation because he must attend a 15-day continuous training period each year, a weekly training night and about one weekend in three. Most employers realize the benefit to the nation, themselves and society in general – but not all have any real idea of how dedicated and professional the RMR really is in a modern warfare context.

Every recruit must undergo about two years' training in order to complete the tough Commando course (at CTCRM Lympstone) and it is after this period that final selection for officer training (a further two years) takes place. Once trained, the marine reservist joins his detachment's Commando Company and is able to train as a specialist in one of many fields including Mountain and Arctic

Warfare (M&AW). The initial service is four years with re-engagement until 50 years of age.

RMR SPECIALIST UNITS

2 Raiding Squadron Royal Marines (Reserve) [2 RSRM(R)] was formed in 1978 as a fully-fledged Raiding Squadron which, unlike its regular sister units, is equipped with inflatable raiding craft – the Avon/Dunlop Gemini – powered by 40 hp Johnson engines and other outboard motors. This difference of equipment enables the squadron to operate by different means and in different roles to that of the regular Corps and this is a useful addition to the order of battle.

Detachments are based at all RMR units, and the Headquarters element is at RMR City of London. Transportation is generally provided by Bedford RL 4-tonne trucks in which the Gemini can be easily stowed.

4 Special Boat Section (Reserve) [4 SBS(R)] has the closest RMR connection with the regular special force, which has proved both long and useful. 4 SBS(R) acts in support of the regular squadrons and trains highly-skilled swimmer-canoeist frogmen and parachutists. Like the regulars, these men can approach their objectives by parachute, submarine, canoe or by swimming, in order to carry out a mission.

608 Tactical Air Control Party (Reserve) [608 TACP(R)] at RMR Bristol is a four-man team led by a subaltern, which provides air liaison to land forces and an aircraft control facility in forward areas. In 1979 this team deployed to Belize with a Regular Army battalion on a Regular Arms Plot Tour. This was the first time that a Reserve or Territorial Army Unit had done this work and 608 TACP(R) carried out a further tour in 1981.

The RMR offers the opportunity for civilians to undertake arduous training in parachuting, skiing and cliff climbing which would otherwise not be possible in their normal occupations. In addition, volunteers can specialize as Assault Engineers, Signallers, PT Instructors, Cooks or in supporting weapons (mortars) or platoon weapons.

Royal Marines Reserve officers and men are frequently detached to the regular Corps and occasionally to units of the Royal Netherlands Marine Corps and United States Marine Corps (with whom the Royal Marines have close liaisons) for exercise purposes. Such training has recently been carried out in Belize, Canada, Cyprus, Hong Kong, the Netherlands and Norway. There are also opportunities for Staff College training and, indeed, senior officers must pass a Staff College course before taking up their appointments. The RMR units are commanded by an officer of Lieutenant Colonel rank.

COMMANDO UNITS

The fighting strength of the Royal Marines is 3 Commando Brigade (3 Cdo Bde) which is made up of three operational units known as the Commandos. 40 Cdo is trained for Temperate Climate Operations, while the other two units are concerned primarily with Mountain & Arctic Warfare – 42 Commando (Cdo) and 45 Cdo Group.

40 COMMANDO

40 Commando Royal Marines took part in the Dieppe raid in August 1942 having been formed as A Commando the preceding February. More than half the unit was saved from being wiped out in Dieppe by the gallant action of the then CO, Lieutenant Colonel J.P. Phillipps. In July 1943, the action was still amphibious assault, but the venue was now Sicily and later the mainland of Italy, before moving across to Yugoslavia and the Adriatic islands.

After the Second World War there was very little respite for the unit, as it was involved in internal security operations in Palestine (now Israel), including peace-keeping between Jews and Arabs at Haifa docks, being the last British unit to leave the Mandate on independence. After the Near East came Hong Kong and Malaya, before returning to the Suez Canal Zone for yet more internal security operations.

The increase of terrorist activity in Cyprus by the EOKA bands led to 40 Commando being deployed to the island in 1955, using helicopters for the first time in an urban anti-terrorist role. Dogs were also used to good effect. The unit was involved in the Suez campaign, but did not have its final tour of Cyprus until 1959. After training in Malta, the unit moved to Malaya in 1962, spending almost ten years in the Far East in anti-terrorist operations in Malaya and Borneo.

In November 1971, Four Zero was the last unit to leave Singapore and it moved back to the United Kingdom as part of the then Labour government's disbandment of the East of Suez role. In January 1972, 40 Cdo was re–established in Seaton Barracks, Plymouth before setting off for an operational tour in Northern Ireland.

Cyprus was again the venue for the unit when it went as the

Spearhead Battalion to cover the withdrawal of British civilians and to maintain the peace during the Turkish invasion and subsequent partition of the island in 1974. In March 1979, 40 Commando undertook a year's tour as the garrison battalion at Ballykelly, near Londonderry.

For Operation Corporate, 40 Cdo was the first Royal Marines Commando ashore at San Carlos, where the unit was in charge of the beachhead. A and C companies, plus the support weapons, went to Bluff Cove to reinforce the 1st Battalion Welsh Guards which had suffered so badly after the bombing of *Sir Galahad* and *Sir Tristram*. The remainder of the Commando took the Argentine surrender on West Falkland. After the Falklands, it was back to Northern Ireland and peace–keeping in Cyprus as part of the United Nations force and a six months deployment to Belize.

42 COMMANDO

Formed from the 1st Battalion Royal Marines in October 1943, 42 Commando has a long line of tradition and battle honours, including the capture of Belle Isle (1761), the American War of Independence (1775-76), the Crimea (1850), China (1857) and Egypt (1882). During the First World War, 1st Battalion RM took part in the Gallipoli campaign, as well as fighting in the trenches of Flanders and France.

A ski patrol of 42 Cdo prepares to deplane from a Sea King helicopter of 846 Naval Air Squadron supporting the Commando in Norway. The skiers are armed with the new SA 80 rifle which is apparently popular for travelling by helicopter and on skis (Patrick Allen).

By the late 1930s, the Royal Marines Brigade (which included 1st Bn RM) was a fully armed and ready unit which when war came was held in reserve to defend the United Kingdom against invasion. At this time 1st Bn was manned by marines from the Chatham Division of the Royal Marines and to this day, 42 Cdo wear the distinctive white lanyard of the 1st Bn adopted at this time.

When it was reorganized in 1943, 42 Commando (as the Battalion became known) undertook defence of the United Kingdom duties for a short time and one of its claims to fame was that Evelyn Waugh, the novelist, was a company commander at one time. After training in Scotland, 42 Cdo sailed for India to form part of the 3rd Special Service Brigade for operations against the Japanese. After stopping in Ceylon (now Sri Lanka), the Commando took part in the amphibious landings down the coast of Burma, and on 31 January 1945 the unit achieved fame by holding Hill 170 against a very heavy Japanese counter assault and artillery bombardment. The hill was the key to holding of Kangaw beachhead and Kangaw Day, a remembrance of this epic battle, is celebrated annually by the unit.

After the War, 42 Commando was diverted from garrison duties in Penang (Malaya) to Hong Kong to assist in the guarding of Japanese prisoners of war and assist in the normalization of the Colony. This operation was as part of 3 Commando Brigade Royal Marines and as part of the Brigade, Four Two moved to Malta in July 1947, only to return to Hong Kong in August 1949 to counter any invasion threat during the first days of the newly-created People's Republic of China next door. The unit spent less than a year in Hong Kong before moving off to Malaya where a state of emergency had been declared in 1950.

From June 1950 to May 1952, 42 Commando was operational in Malaya, based mainly in Ipoh, and undertook 22 months of active service including a number of highly gallant engagements.

The next two years were spent in the Near East, based in Malta but training in Tripoli and deployed to the Suez Canal Zone. However, with the run-down Royal Marines numbers, 42 Commando was returned home reduced to an operational nucleus to run the selection and training courses at Bickleigh, Plymouth, but this did not stop the Commando from being deployed overseas for Suez (1956) and the Lebanon Crisis (1958).

42 Commando was selected to man the new Commando Carrier, *Bulwark*, and arrived aboard with the ship in Singapore in June 1960. The ship and its commandos worked together in a number of

training exercises until called into action in July 1961, coming to the aid of Kuwait which expected invasion by Iraq at any time.

In December 1962, the unit was in Singapore and sent to put down the revolt in Brunei, after which the new Commando Carrier, *Albion*, embarked the Commando. It was used as a floating base for Army and RM forces to operate against Indonesian insurgents during the Confrontation period when 42 Cdo worked ashore as an infantry battalion. After Borneo and Malaysia, it was Aden where 42 Commando guarded and secured the orderly withdrawal of British troops in December 1967.

The new Assault Ships, *Fearless* and *Intrepid*, had been commissioned during this time and 42 Cdo was engaged in exercises throughout the Far East and the NATO area until 31 March 1971.

The terrorist troubles in Northern Ireland were very evident and 42 Commando based at Bickleigh was deployed to the Province in various groupings during the period to 1971/77, including participation in Operation Motorman. The 1970s saw the Commando exercising its NATO role with deployments to Canada, the Caribbean and the United States.

In February 1978, the Commando began its acquaintance with the Mountain & Arctic Warfare role, but Four Two was also deployed to South Armagh's 'bandit country', to Hong Kong in an anti-illegal immigrant role and to the tropical New Hebrides islands (now Vanuatu) to quell a rebellion of dissident tribesmen in 1980. In 1982, elements of 42 Cdo were responsible for the liberation of South Georgia and Southern Thule, as well as participating in battles for Mount Kent and Mount Harriet on the Falkland Islands 'proper'.

45 COMMANDO GROUP

45 Commando Group was formed on 1 April 1971 and established at Condor Base, the former Royal Naval Air Station at Arbroath on the North Sea coast of Scotland. The Group comprises 45 Commando Royal Marines (details of 1945-71 service can be found on page 20) and Whiskey Company (Royal Netherlands Marine Corps), 7 (Spinx) Commando Light Battery (Royal Artillery), Condor Troop of 59 Independent Commando Squadron (Royal Engineers) and several smaller ancillary units.

Whiskey Company of the Royal Netherlands Marine Corps (RNLMC) is the equivalent in size of a reinforced RM rifle com-

All Commandos serving in Norway are practised on skis, like Mne Chris Penny of Z Company, 45 Cdo Gp, photographed at the mountain-top command post.

pany and as a result of intensive co-operation between Britain and the Netherlands in NATO, the Company is attached to 45 Cdo Grp for the majority of the year. The assignment was carried out in October 1972 and the unit now trains in Scotland and Norway alongside the British marines.

Condor Troop is the only independent troop of 59 Ind Cdo Sqn and is specialist in Mountain & Arctic Warfare operations (see also page 60).

Because 45 Cdo already has X-ray, Yankee and Zulu companies, it was decided in 1973 to call 13 Company RNLMC, Whiskey Company, during its time under command of 45 Cdo Group. Somehow, one imagines that this name appealed to the 'Cloggies' as the Dutch are usually known! Whiskey Company has its own force of US Navy-design landing craft which are also deployed to Norway.

Larger than the other two Commandos, 45 Cdo Gp is commanded by a Lieutenant Colonel who is also the CO of 45 Cdo RM, having some 1,000 all ranks in the Group. The Group is assigned to the NATO Northern Region role and was the United Kingdom's first Mountain & Arctic Warfare unit in December 1969, since when it has acted as the land force element of the UK's contribution to the defence of the 'northern flank' of Norway.

SPECIALIST UNITS

Although the Royal Marines is itself part of the British special forces and considered to be an elite element in the British and NATO order of battle, the Corps still has a number of specialist units which support Commando Forces wherever they are called upon to operate.

Commando Logistic Regiment: supplies all logistical needs.

Comacchio Group: protects British oil installations.

Mountain & Arctic Warfare Cadre: the mountain leaders.

Raiding Squadrons: put people ashore at the right spot.

539 Assault Squadron: operates independently beyond enemy lines.

Special Boat Squadron: secures beaches and provides intelligence.

Commando Brigade Air Squadron: highly flexible anti-tank force.

Landing Craft Company: supplies waterborne transport.

Ships' Detachments: support the Royal Navy at sea.

Band Service: provides ceremonial and medical assistance.

COMMANDO LOGISTIC REGIMENT

To provide a complete logistical support function for 3 Commando Brigade, the Commando Logistic Regiment was formed between July 1971 and January 1972, using the logistic skills in the support elements of 3 Cdo Bde and some administrative elements from Commando Forces. By 1982, the organization had grown to embody seven different British Army, Royal Navy and Royal Marines cap badges in time to play a vital role in Operation Corporate.

The Commando Logistic Regiment has four basic roles at home and for Brigade-size operations anywhere in the world:

> To provide transport support;
> To provide medical support;
> To provide ordnance support;
> To provide workshop facilities for Commando Forces.

To fulfil the role, the Regiment is organized into five squadrons for administrative and operational reasons.

Headquarters Squadron provides the Command & Control through the Regimental Headquarters (RHQ) and administrative

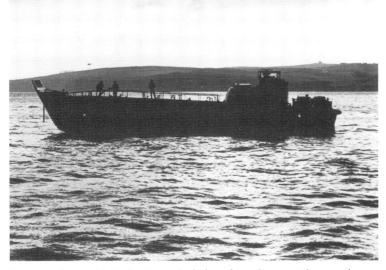

Support is often provided by landing craft which can be used to re-supply units ashore as well as in what is regarded as the more traditional — but declining — amphibious assault role (RM/A1 Campell).

elements of the Regiment through the medium of the Echelon. When deployed operationally the RHQ becomes the Headquarters of the Brigade Maintenance Area (BMA) to control all the functions of the BMA and to implement the logistical plan of the Brigade Headquarters.

Transport Squadron, based at RM Coypool, Devon, is responsible for second line support of Commando Forces and their attached elements. It involves the movement of material between the beach support area, brigade maintenance area, distributive points or units of combat supplies and stores. In addition, the squadron provides vehicles for troop movement over any terrain. During training periods in the United Kingdom, the Squadron provides a second line transport capability for Commando Forces.

Medical Squadron is manned by Royal Naval personnel all of whom have been trained to Commando standard and all of whom wear the coveted green beret. In barracks the Squadron is responsible for the day-to-day medical requirements based around Plymouth and the Royal Marines Barracks, Stonehouse. In the field, when deployed operationally or for training, the Squadron provides the first and second line medical support to operational units, including the evacuation of casualties from the Regimental Aid

Although Royal Marines are used to 'yomping', the standing mode of transport in Norway is the Volvo Bv 202 caterpillar-tracked vehicle, seen here disembarking from an LCU of 539 Assault Squadron RM (Robin Adshead).

Posts and all medical support prior to a casualty being transferred to a hospital.

Ordnance Squadron carries out four important roles: the bulk distribution of ammunition, petroleum products and rations for Commando Forces; the holding 'on wheels' of a two months' supply of motor transport and technical stores to maintain all Commando Forces' unit requirements; provision of Combat Supply troops to carry out stock control in the BMA and at Distribution Points; provision of local resources teams for the purchase of locally-obtained stores, whether on exercise or when operationally deployed.

Workshop Squadron based with Transport Squadron at Coypool provides vehicle, electronic, instrument and general second line repair facilities for the Commando Forces. Amongst its other tasks are the recovery of light vehicles and the provision of an Oversnow Troop with particular responsibility for the Royal Marines Volvo Bv202 fleet of vehicles.

FALKLANDS EXPERIENCE

The Falklands conflict was of special significance to the Commando Logistic Regiment because it proved that the systems and procedures worked out in the large number of peacetime exercises prior to 1982 were sound. Operation Corporate was a conflict which if not won by superior logistical support was one which could so easily have been lost because spares, ammunition, fuel and other necessities were not delivered to the right people at the right time.

Some 335 all ranks out of 600 men were deployed to the Falkland Islands during the conflict and the Regiment set up a special base at Ajax Bay on San Carlos Water. The BMA was constituted around the now famous disused refrigeration plant in an area of 400 sq m (4,305 sq ft) and, later, with the arrival of 5th Infantry Brigade, the BMA became the Divisional Maintenance Area.

During the progression of the British advance on Port Stanley, the Commando Logistic Regiment established two forward BMAs at Teal Inlet and Fitzroy, the latter with elements of the British Army's 81 and 91 Ordnance Companies, Royal Army Ordnance Corps.

A main dressing station run by the Medical Squadron was set up at Ajax Bay in the refrigeration plant and at Teal Inlet a forward dressing station was established. The Squadron was augmented by three Royal Naval Surgical Support Teams, two of which stayed afloat in the transport ships for hospital and medical duties, including evacuation. Some 1,000 casualties passed through the hands of the Squadron, yet only three men died under second line treatment, a major achievement for a combat situation.

Also at Ajax Bay, the Workshop Squadron undertook the major defence of the BMA, and the burial of the dead, and constructed second line maintenance facilities. To ease the burden of work and to give a better service the Squadron also deployed elements to the major formations in the field to perform immediate second line repairs. This helped to keep the British forces in Operation Corporate mobile.

During the conflict, Commando Logistic Regiment moved over 9,000 tonnes of stores, received one dead and 26 wounded through air attack and earned two OBEs and four Mentions in Despatches.

After the cessation of fighting on the Islands, the Regiment moved into Port Stanley to consolidate, and to facilitate the recovery operations during the after-conflict clean-up.

COMACCHIO GROUP

In order to protect the vital interests of British offshore oil and gas

Comacchio Group is the UK response to terrorism offshore on the many oil and natural gas platforms. A favourite mode of transport is the helicopter (RN).

installations in the North and Celtic Seas, the Royal Marines has had a specialist role since 1977. Today, Comacchio Group, based at Arbroath, Scotland provides a full range of protection and intervention skills to deter terrorist and other unfriendly acts, as well as to secure the installations, by force if necessary.

In July 1977, 42 Commando's L Company was the first unit to be deployed in what was then called the 'oilsafe' programme and other companies were later trained in the skills necessary to protect an oil installation from attack or to liberate one. In May 1980, with the continued development of the offshore hydrocarbon industry and the greater risk of terrorism, the Royal Marines formed Comacchio Company with seven rifle troops of 32 men each. This number was later increased and by 1984, Comacchio Company had become Comacchio Group. Another change took place in 1988.

The Royal Marines attached to Comacchio Group have been trained in a number of ways of reaching the offshore installation, including abseiling from a Sea King HAS 5 helicopter of 819 Naval Air Squadron or a Gazelle from 3 Cdo Bde Air Sqn, in swimming from a submarine or small craft or parachuting from an RAF transport aircraft.

MOUNTAIN & ARCTIC WARFARE CADRE

Members of the Royal Marines Mountain & Arctic Warfare (M & AW) Cadre are the survival specialists of 3 Cdo Bde RM, trained to

The Royal Navy's Sea King HC 4 can be used for night and adverse weather insertions (RM/PO Phot Campbell).

operate and live behind enemy lines. Qualified members of the Cadre are known as Mountain Leaders (MLs), a qualification earned after nine months of gruelling training in Devon, Cornwall and the Outer Hebrides. Candidates for this course are already fully-qualified Royal Marines.

When the first Royal Marine commandos of 45 Cdo arrived in northern Norway in January 1970 for Arctic Warfare training, the special relationship between the Corps and Norway began. RM soldiers had been to Norway before, including 41 Cdo in 1968, but 45 Cdo was designated the Arctic Warfare group from 1970. In August 1971, the first Alpine courses were begun, leading to an increasing number of M & AW specialist NCOs and officers who now form the Cadre.

The main role of the Mountain & Arctic Warfare Cadre is the long range reconnaissance of Alpine and Arctic regions, often acting as leaders for the Arctic-trained members of 45 and other Cdo groups, as well as troops from the British and other NATO armies. The Cadre achieved fame for the daylight attack on Top Malo House on East Falkland during the advance on Port Stanley, when they defeated an Argentine special forces unit holding one of the last enemy special forces' position west of the mountains around the Falklands' capital.

The Cadre headquarters are at Plymouth in the Citadel garrison, where 25 candidates are selected for each training course. During the M & AW training course, the rank of all candidates is suspen-

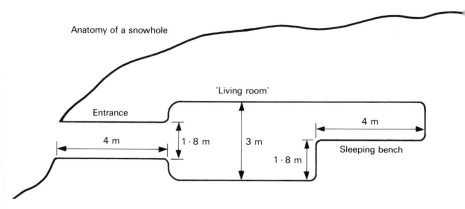

Anatomy of a snowhole

ded, and they are expected to show the specialist qualities needed to remain isolated behind the lines. These qualities have been des-cribed as 'badger-like' by Major General Julian Thompson, who as a Brigadier commanded 3 Cdo Bde in the Falklands; MLs must learn to switch off any feelings of discomfort but retain their keen military and tactical senses which could save their lives.

They have to be mentally and physically fit for the course for such evolutions as carrying a 120 lb (54 kg) pack for 90 miles (145 km), clearing the infamous 'Land's End Long Jump' 270 ft (82 m) above the sea before moving on to rock climbing. After one month on course, the candidates are expected to attempt a night climb without lights and later without ropes. For fun, they learn to abseil 200 ft (61 m) from a helicopter and by the end of the course, the candidates would be expected to climb anything in front of them.

One of the most important survival lessons taught to all Arctic-trained RM Commandos is the use of the snowhole. In hard-packed snow, a 13 x 6 ft (4 x 1.8 m) entrance is cut into the snow to create a living space for two or four men, who rest on shelves cut 6 ft (1.8 m) above the floor level because cold air sinks to the floor level. Also provided for in the snowhole is cooking by petrol stove, air circula-tion through a system of vents and the sleeping shelves are fur-nished with polystyrene sleeping mats.

RAIDING SQUADRONS

To develop the abilities of small craft and to provide a corps of specialists to support the operations of the Special Boat Squadron

For assault and reconnaissance operations, especially in Norway, the Corps uses the Dell Quay Rigid Raider. These sturdy boats are well-designed for all sorts of operations, including driving out of water and up the beach to land marines 'without getting their feet wet' (Dell Quay).

and Mountain & Arctic Warfare Cadre special forces, the Royal Marines formed its first raiding squadrons in 1970, closely allied to Landing Craft Company.

1 Raiding Squadron RM was formed in 1970, under the control of Landing Craft Company, but operational control passed to the Cdo Logistic Regiment. 2 Raiding Squadron RM was also formed in 1970 but disbanded in 1972, only to be reformed in 1979 as 2 Raiding Squadron RMR working from the United Kingdom. 3 Raiding Squadron was raised in 1980 for operations, initially with Rigid Raiding craft, later Avon Seariders, around Hong Kong to assist with the capture of illegal immigrants and later to apprehend drug smugglers. It was disbanded in 1988 and its role turned over to the Royal Hong Kong Police.

Operational expertise in the Norwegian winter and for the last decade in the waters around Hong Kong has given the Royal Marines a special skill with small, powered craft which is much admired around the world. To support regular deployments to Norway and to form an important specialist group in wartime, 1 RSRM has an Arctic Warfare Section which has been working to develop raiding craft tactics and which is now under the operational control of 539 Assault Squadron RM.

The principal craft of raiding are the Dell Quay Rigid Raider, the Avon Searider and the Avon or Dunlop Gemini inflatable craft, the

Despite the retention of the larger Assault ships, the independent landing craft will remain an important asset in Norway. This is Brown Sow, one of the LCU Mk 9s used as mother craft for rigid raiders of 539 Assault Sqn RM and as a transport in its own right. It is pictured at Torvik Beach, Norway.

latter being capable of use from a conventional submarine. Trials are now being carried out with a new type of semi-inflatable raiding craft. In addition, it is possible to mount extremely successful operations from LCVPs and other landing craft, or to take up craft from trade for the purpose.

Crews of Raiding Squadrons are often detached in sections to work directly with Commandos and other Commando Forces units. In the 1970s an Arctic Warfare Section of 1 RSRM was formed and specialist equipment has been designed for and issued to the coxswains of this section. Each Raiding Craft section has a specialist maintenance unit attached to keep the high speed craft in top condition during exercises or on operational service.

539 ASSAULT SQUADRON

This is one of the British armed forces' newest units, having been formed in 1983 as a direct result of the experience gained during the Falklands conflict, which reinforced the trials carried out in 1971 by 45 Cdo during an exercise. The tactics developed in 1971 were successfully used in the South Atlantic.

539 Asslt Sqn is commanded by a senior Major, being formed by Major Ewen Southby-Tailyour OBE RM, one of the leaders of the

Above *Leith in South Georgia, April 1982. This was the scene of the Royal Marines' first success in the South Atlantic war when 42 Cdo's M Company liberated the island from Argentine control (HMS Plymouth Flight).*

Below *Starting forth on an exercise reconnaissance of enemy installations, a swimmer/canoeist from the Special Boat Squadron shows the close co-operation between the Royal Navy's Submarine Service and the Corps (RM).*

Above A marine from the Mountain & Arctic Warfare Cadre of the Royal Marines mans an observation post during a temporate climate exercise. Like the SBS, the M&AW Cadre is equipped with the US-pattern M-16 rifle (RM).

Below A ski patrol with attendant Bv 202 oversnow vehicle, known as a 'bandwagon' to the Corps, illustrates a typical scene in Norway (RM).

Above *The Landing Ship Logistic, RFA Sir Lancelot, moves in towards a beach on the Dorset coast during an amphibious exercise. These ships are vital to the beach landing capability of the Royal Marines, yet are manned by a civilian crew (RN/HMS Osprey).*

Below *A typical peacetime training environment of the Royal Marines is Dartmoor, the location of this view of a Sea King HC 4 commando support helicopter from 846 Naval Air Squadron, based at RNAS Yeovilton (RN/HMS Heron).*

Above A 'stick' of commandos arrive at a landing zone in northern Norway and collect their equipment, including skis, prior to a patrol. The helicopter provides an important means of moving troops around Norway (Cdo Forces News Team/CPO Pete Holdgate).

Below The 3rd Commando Brigade Air Squadron, Royal Marines, flies two light battlefield helicopter types of which the Lynx AH 1 is the only one armed. It carries up to eight TOW wire-guided anti-tank missiles (Westland).

1971 exercise. OC 539 has the additional role of being the landing craft adviser to Commodore Amphibious Warfare (COMAW) and the Commander 3 Cdo Bde. The peacetime complement of the unit is:

3 Landing Craft Utility (LCU), new construction and Arctic equipped;

4 Landing Craft Vehicles & Personnel (LCVP);

23 Dell Quay Rigid Raiders;

23 Avon Gemini inflatable raiding craft.

In wartime, various additional units are added to the strength of the Squadron, including extra LCUs (from the Assault Ship *Fearless* or *Intrepid*, the mexifloats from the *Sir Galahad* type Landing Ships Logistic (LSL) and allied equipment, such as the Landing Craft Assault (LCAs) manned by the Royal Netherlands Marine Corps.

The LCUs have been deployed across the North Sea to Norway under their own power, and recent highly successful trials with the 'Black Pig' and the 'Brown Sow' have shown that a small group of well-provided and trained landing craft can remain camouflaged by day and operate by night with great success in Norwegian waters. The Arctic style LCUs (which are capable of taking the latest British main battle tanks) would act as mother ships for operations which require the smaller LCVPs, Rigid Raiders and Gemini inflatables.

The small craft, such as the Rigid Raiders, can be delivered close to the objective by Sea King HC 4 helicopter, which carries the 'raiders' in its cabin, ready to abseil to the waiting Rigid Raider below when the initial point is reached. Like the Special Boat Squadron, with whom 539 work closely, the favoured method of delivering the Avon Gemini craft is to use a submarine or landing craft. The crews of the raiding craft are obviously Commando trained and can operate as part of a raiding force. During the 1987 exercise, the Squadron proved that raiding operations, using the LCVP and small craft, could be carried out up to 200 nm (370 km) from the mother ship. The new LCVPs can move at 20 kt (37 km/h) with a string of Rigid Raiders in tow, the crews and raiding parties being rested in the landing craft during the passage. On reaching the objective, the rigid raiders are deployed and the LCVP hides-up in a fjord or island before recovering the crews and raiders and moving back to the mother ship. Aboard the mother ship there is special accommodation, feeding and clothing-drying facilities for such an operation.

Not many pictures are taken of the Special Boat Squadron, but this publicity picture shows a swimmer-canoeist with his Klepper canoe. Note the US-pattern M-16 rifle, a favourite weapon of the SBS (RM).

SPECIAL BOAT SQUADRON

The Admiralty decided to raise the Special Boat Squadron (SBS) to provide a nucleus of unconventional and specialist warfare knowledge for amphibious and other wartime operations. Today the SBS has an enviable reputation for excellence, but has never courted the rather elitist persona of the Special Air Service, its British Army equivalent although there is a good working relationship.

Its operations during the Second World War include various beach reconnaissance sorties, forays to mine enemy shipping and covert surveillance and reporting operations, many behind enemy lines. Since the War, the Squadron has been active in many places where the Royal Marines have fought, and operations include the parachuting of a specialist team to the Cunard liner, *Queen Elizabeth 2*, when a terrorist group was suspected of placing explosives aboard in May 1972.

In the 1980s, the SBS has not changed its role significantly and it maintains a cloak of anonymity over its operations, training and function. Officially nothing is reported or commented on concerning the Squadron, but it is thought that the roles of the SAS and SBS are similar (though not identical), with the latter generally keeping to the maritime sphere, moving to its objective by some form of seaborne transport. It is known, however, that the peacetime role, besides training for conflict, now includes anti-terrorist planning or operations linked to maritime scenarios, such as liner, oil rig or port hijack.

The SBS today is about the size of an infantry rifle company with specialists in technical skills attached, especially to assist with telecommunications and logistics. For operations, the Squadron would be split into smaller units and be made available to the local theatre commander for intelligence gathering and sabotage tasks.

RECRUITMENT
Royal Marines, officers and men, are selected from within the Corps and so start with the background of above average physical skills, military abilities and high intellect. The recruits undergo another selection process as hard as if not harder than their original enlistment.

The lucky few (less than 50 per cent of the candidates) who pass a two-week selection will have to have demonstrated to the Squadron that they possess the physical ability for the many demanding tasks and the mental strength to operate alone, and to combat the claustrophobia induced by underwater work in pitch blackness.

The specialization of the SBS operative, although not exclusively his, is that of swimmer/canoeist, but a marine in the Squadron will cross-train in communications (patrol signaller), applied first aid (paramedic) or skier (mountain leader/ski instructor). First, though, the SBS specialist will need to learn how to conduct himself in the water as a swimmer, diver and boat handler.

TRAINING FOR THE ELITE'S ELITE
A typical training sortie might include a submerged approach to a 'guarded' beach which involves swimming undetected for over a mile, using only a compass and depth gauge for navigation. The swimmer, perhaps launched from a submerged conventional submarine, will be using the standard oxygen rebreath sub-aqua system and carrying specialist kit for reconnaissance, sabotage or assassination. If he is not completely at home in the water he will not fit into the Squadron.

Having mastered swimming, the SBS recruit develops his skills in boats and light craft, including the famous Klepper Aerius canoe, a German-built design which has been in use for many years. Klepper

Royal Marines placing charges on a railway line, another typical Special Boat Squadron operation of disruption behind enemy lines. In the Falklands, the SBS provided important intelligence and reconnaissance information, demonstrating more of their talents (RM).

canoes can be launched from various craft including landing craft and partially submerged submarines. They are one of the SBS's favourite modes of transport because of their stealthy approach to a stand-off launch point, giving the team a better chance than a noisy aircraft arrival. The canoeist will have to navigate across open water, approach guarded harbour locations with stealth and come ashore through rocks and raging surf. A typical open water journey may be as much as 30 nm (56 km).

Commando training will already have taught the SBS recruit how to move and fight on land, but the SBS needs people who can cross country, reach an objective, gain intelligence and return to the coast without being seen. Crossing land, the SBS pride themselves on carrying large loads of equipment over great distances, as well as being able to blend in with their surroundings.

SBS recruits have to be skilled with all weapons from the Standard Royal Marines armoury which they might have occasion to use, as well as more specialist weapons, from sniper rifles to anti-tank missile launchers. The SBS operator uses other weapons which his colleagues in the SAS have also found useful, such as the famous Heckler & Kock sub-machine pistol. Besides weapons there are communication sets, such as satellite radio systems, and demolition charges.

The basic operational grouping for the Special Boat Squadron is the section, led by a Sergeant who has graduated to the status of

Embarked on the light aircraft carrier, HMS Invincible, these TOW-armed Westland Lynx helicopters from 3 Commando Brigade Air Squadron represent an important and flexible anti-tank force for such areas of Norway (RN/Invincible/PO Kent).

Swimmer/Canoeist First Class (SC1) through a series of specialist courses, including further training at the Commando Training Centre, Royal Marines at Lympstone, Devon. His second-in-command will probably be an SC2 (Corporal) with two SC3 (Marines) to complete the team. Every year, sections train throughout the world, including Arctic training periods in northern Norway where the Royal Marines have a NATO role and the SBS must learn to carry out their specialist role in temperatures down to −40°C.

While Marine Swimmer/Canoeists will generally progress through the hierarchy of the Special Boat Squadron, officers who have passed into this exacting world will be expected to broaden their military and naval experience by completing tours in other parts of the Corps.

The Squadron is, however, very much a 'club' and it is unusual for non-commissioned personnel to spend much of their remaining service life away from the SBS.

COMMANDO BRIGADE AIR SQUADRON

The Royal Marines own helicopter support unit was formed at Dieppe Barracks, Sembawang in Singapore on 12 August 1968 and was titled 3 Commando Brigade Air Squadron Royal Marines, officially shortened to 3 Cdo Bde Air Sqn RM, unofficially to 'the BAS' or 'Brigade Air Squadron' and to many aviation enthusiasts as

CBAS (pronounced Sea Bass).

The initial equipment was the Westland-built Agusta-Bell Model 47 G-3 light observation helicopter called the Sioux AH 1 in Army Air Corps service. The helicopter was already in use with several smaller air troops which were amalgamated into the larger body: Brigade Flight, 40 Cdo RM Air Trp, 42 Cdo RM Air Trp and 29 Cdo Lt Regt RA Air Observation Post (AOP) Trp. To supplement the Sioux helicopters, the Westland Scout AH 1 was brought into service in 1970.

When the Royal Marines departed from Singapore in 1971, the Squadron reorganized absorbing the remaining independent air troops of 41 and 45 Cdos at the same time. The reorganized Squadron, commanded by a Major RM, had an anti-tank flight of four Westland Scout AH 1 armed with the Nord SS 11 wire-guided anti-tank guided weapon, and fired with the aid of a Ferranti/Avimo AF120 roof-mounted sight. In addition, two utility Scouts were on strength with bulged doors for casualty evacuation.

For reconnaissance, flights of three Sioux AH 1 each usually provided support to a nominated Commando and bore the name of an associated battle honour:

> Brunei Flight (29 Cdo Regt RA)
> Dieppe Flight (40 Cdo RM)
> Kangaw Flight (42 Cdo RM)
> Montforterbeek Flight (45 Cdo RM Gp)
> Salerno Flight (41 Cdo RM)

During 1974-75, the Sioux helicopters were replaced with 12 Westland-built Aerospatiale SA 341 Gazelle AH 1 helicopters for liaison, observation, reconnaissance and evacuation. The Gazelle/Scout mix was operational during Operation Corporate, but by the next winter season in Norway the unit had received six Westland Lynx AH 1 to replace the Scouts. The Lynx is the standard British Army helicopter anti-tank guided weapon system and is armed with the Hughes Aircraft Corporation TOW wire-guided anti-tank missile in its TOW-1, Improved TOW and Further Improved TOW configurations.

The present role of the Squadron, the largest light helicopter squadron in the British forces, is to provide the battlefield liaison, reconnaissance and anti-tank force for 3 Cdo Bde RM. The squadron retains very close links with the Naval Air Commando squadrons of the Royal Navy's Fleet Air Arm co-located at Yeovilton, Somerset and with the Army Air Corps. It is standard policy for

During an exercise on Salisbury Plain, elements of 3 Cdo Bde Air Sqn set up a command post in a field location with well-camouflaged vehicles. The helicopter in the foreground is a Gazelle, used primarily for light observation tasks (Patrick Allen).

pilots and other aircrew to train with the AAC at Middle Wallop because the helicopters used are identical. Montforterbeek Flight is based at Arbroath to support 45 Cdo Gp RM which is also located at Condor Base.

Other fighting arms are represented in the Squadron, including Royal Army Ordnance Corps aircraft spares specialists, Royal Electrical and Mechanical Engineers aircraft technicans and Royal Artillery aircrewmen. Survival equipment is usually in the capable hands of a Royal Navy non-commissioned officer. Royal Marines officers can also undertake exchange tours with the Army Air Corps and the Naval Air Commando squadrons; recently one has had command of 845 Naval Air Squadron, equipped with the Sea King HC 4.

OPERATION CORPORATE
The light helicopters operated in the Falkland Islands were drawn from 3 Cdo Bde Air Sqn RM and 656 Squadron Army Air Corps, both equipped with the Gazelle AH 1 for observation and the Scout AH 1 for general utility and anti-tank guided weapon support. The Scout was used for night re-supply and casualty evacuation duties rather than as a missile carrier because the Argentine forces did not possess armour – although it is said that 'sangars' used by the Argentine forces were attacked with a 90 per cent success rate, only one missile going 'rogue' with a wire break. One sangar was found to contain an Argentine 105 mm howitzer position, thankfully neutralized by the helicopters.

Royal Marines Gazelles were fitted with the Thomson-Brandt SNEB 68 mm and the MATRA 68 mm rocket pods after trials in the

In the 1970s, the Royal Marines equipped with the Aerospatiale Gazelle AH 1 helicopter which has proved to be very adaptable for land-based and embarked operations. Here a Gazelle from C Flight, 3 Cdo Bde Air Sqn, lands on HMS Fearless. Note the LCUs and LSL in the background.

United Kingdom with Army Air Corps helicopters. The SNEB was intended as an area suppression weapon, but even after successful firings over Ascension Island on the way south, the weapons were not used in anger. They were, however, considered to be a major morale booster.

Most of the helicopters travelled to the South Atlantic as deck cargo in the six 'Sir Bedevere' Class LSL (Landing Ships Logistic) and some suffered short-term salt-water corrosion.

Four Royal Marines flights were allocated to the landings at San Carlos:

A Flight: a Gazelle to support HQ 3 Cdo Bde and two helicopters to support 29 Cdo Regt in reconnaissance and gunnery control.

B Flight: a utility Scout to support HQ 3 Cdo Bde and two SS 11 armed Scouts for both 40 Cdo and 45 Cdo.

C Flight: allocated two Gazelles armed with SNEB to escort the Sea King HC 4 helicopters of 846 Squadron and to clear any anti-aircraft positions or the landing zones. These helicopters were also armed with the 7.62 mm GPMG (General Purpose Machine Gun) but two were lost immediately prior to the landings, when supporting 846 Squadron.

M Flight: three Gazelles were kept in readiness to support 42 Cdo.

Torvik beach, during one of the Cold Winter exercise series in Norway. The landing craft is approaching a beach-head controlled by HMS Fearless' Beach Assault Unit. The trackway to the local road is kept open by the Michigan tractor at the water's edge.

Amongst the operations undertaken by the Gazelles and Scouts of the Squadron were the support of the Special Air Service and the Special Boat Squadron in covert operations, the casualty evacuation of Parachute Regiment personnel from Goose Green and the move towards Teal. After that it was towards Port Stanley that all operations were directed and the RM helicopters supported the efforts of 42 and 45 Commandos (with 3 Bn Parachute Regt) to take Mount Kent and Mount Harriet as well as the Two Sisters by re-supplying inbound and 'casevacing' outbound. A Royal Marine from C Flight was the first British helicopter back into Port Stanley after the ceasefire, taking senior officers for a parley.

During the conflict the Gazelles flew a total of more than 1,322 hours and Scouts nearly 790 hours; other than those destroyed, the individual helicopters flew more than 100 hours each and one Gazelle over 200 hours.

LANDING CRAFT COMPANY

The specialist amphibious assault ships (LPDs) of the Royal Navy – *Fearless* and *Intrepid* – carry landing craft which are manned exclusively by the Royal Marines of Landing Craft Company. The whole branch is controlled from Royal Marines Poole via the sponsorship of each ship's Commanding Officer. Landing Craft Company is responsible for the training of crews for the LCVPs (Landing Craft Vehicle and Personnel) on the LPDs' davits and the LCUs (Landing Craft Utility).

To ensure smooth administration, Landing Craft Assault Squadrons are attached to *Fearless* (4 Assault Squadron) and *Intrepid* (6 Assault Squadron) whilst a third squadron is available for other duties, including its use aboard STUFT (Ships Taken Up From Trade) shipping.

Aboard the LPDs, there are four LCUs and each 12-tonne craft is crewed by a Corporal and two Marines. The LPDs are equipped to carry four LCUs in the dock-type compartment beneath their flight decks and they operate in and out of this when the ship is 'flooded down' close inshore. Wheeled and tracked equipment, as well as palletted loads are transferred from the ship's vehicle decks into the holds of the LCUs and LCVPs in the calm water of the flooded dock. Raiding and other small craft can use the dock as well.

Events in the South Atlantic led to a reappraisal of the Landing Craft element of Royal Marines and as a result a special LC Assault Squadron was formed to support Commando Forces.

Landing craft are now seen not only as part of an amphibious group but can also be independent in a concept known as the Forward Landing Craft Operating Base which will enable 3 Commando Brigade to deploy to, for example, Norway, with limited assistance

One of the LCU Mk 9s based at RM Poole, Dorset, brings vehicles of the Commando Logistic Regiment ashore under exercises on the UK's south coast.

from LPDs and other large ships. Concept development work with 'Black Pig' and 'Brown Sow' has proved the viability of making sea voyages in specially-adapted landing craft under their own power. The trip from Scotland to Norway takes about 36 hours.

Also following the Falklands campaign, a series of new, modern technology LCUs and LCVPs were delivered to the Royal Marines, following development work at ATTURM Instow, North Devon. Following experience in Norway, all LCVPs and LCUs can now be 'Arcticized' for operations in adverse weather north of the Arctic Circle. Covers, heaters and specialist navigational equipment have been provided for this role.

Marines who specialize in Landing Craft are at the lowest level qualified to cox Rigid Raiders and Gemini whilst the highest level is the Officer i/c Landing Craft aboard an LPD. Corporals usually provide the cox'ns for LCVPs and LCUs. This use of smaller craft enables Landing Craft Company to provide a nautical element to Comacchio Group (see page 75) and certain waterborne operations in Northern Ireland and the Special Boat Squadron.

A special three-man detachment to Naval Party 8901 in the Falkland Islands was detached from the Company, consisting of a Corporal and two Marines with their Gemini craft. In addition to military tasks, Landing Craft Company is available to provide assistance to the civil power for disaster relief and casualty evacuation. In line with Britain's assistance to friendly Commonwealth and foreign powers, the Company provides men on secondment to the small boats section of the Royal Brunei Malay Regiment.

SHIPS' DETACHMENTS

Whilst almost all vessels of the Royal Navy and Royal Fleet Auxiliary Service have the capability of embarking varying numbers of Royal Marines, there are certain warships which have detachments allocated to them during a commission.

The present Royal Marines Ships' Detachments are commanded by a Sergeant, a Corporal as second i/c and eight marines. Until 1978 there was a system of an officer and 20 marines, but since then warships have become smaller and there is less accommodation available. There are usually between 15 and 19 detachments at sea, depending on the requirements and deployments under way, including anti-aircraft missile detachments with the warships and auxiliaries of the Armilla Patrol in the Persian Gulf. The following

HMS Endurance's *ship's detachment comes ashore in the Falklands in a Gemini inflatible craft* (RM).

warships can carry RM detachments:

Bristol, the new Dartmouth Training Ship, but which in its primary role would not embark a detachment because of the number of cadets and midshipmen aboard.

Endurance, the Ice Patrol Ship, which carries an enlarged detachment commanded by a Lieutenant RM; *Endurance's* detachment put up a spirited defence of South Georgia in April 1982, surrendering without loss.

'Leander' Class frigates, Batch 2 and 3, some of which have the former mortar well plated over to provide accommodation for the 'Royals'. However, the warships of this type which are designated as 'Squadron Leaders' do not carry a detachment.

'Broadsword' Class, Type 22 Batch 1 frigates, again except the 'Squadron Leader'.

'Rothesay' Class frigates.

Falkland Islands Patrol Craft also embark detachments to supplement Naval Party 8901, the permanent cadre in the Islands.

Selection for the embarked detachments is via the regular sea roster although volunteers are welcomed. Training is carried out at RM Poole and HMS *Raleigh*, the naval rating training centre near

Plymouth. At the latter, the Royals complete an eight-week initial seamanship course in four weeks before returning to Poole for re-training in military skills such as weapons, signals and field craft. This is called Pre-Embarkation Training (PET).

Pre-Joining Training (PJT) is carried out at HMS *Cambridge*, the naval gunnery and internal security school at Plymouth where various aspects of naval gunnery are taught.

The length of time which the detachment will spend at sea depends on the warship's deployment, but it is thought that most warships deploying on guardship duties in areas such as the Carib-bean or Gibraltar carry a detachment. Mention has already been made of the Armilla Patrol detachments who are armed with the Shorts Javelin shoulder-launched guided missile. The generally expected role of the detachments is to form the nucleus of a naval shore party charged with defending British interests, rescuing those threatened by illegal armed action and preserving law and order at the request of a friendly government until other forces arrive.

The standard weapons carried include the personal machine guns, self-loading rifles and pistols of every Royal Marine, as well as larger support weapons such as the LAW 80. Clansman radios are also carried for shore-to-ship communications or they communi-cate with the ship's inflatable boats which are generally manned by the Royals.

ROYAL MARINES BAND SERVICE

Professional music for the Royal Navy is provided by the bands of the Royal Marines, headquartered at the Corps's School of Music at Deal, Kent. Royal Marine Bands have the official title 'Band of Her Majesty's Royal Marines . . . '

The following bands were in commission in 1986:
School of Music, based at Deal;
Commander-in-Chief Naval Home Command
(CINCNAVHOME), based at Eastney, near Portsmouth;
Commander-in-Chief Fleet (CINCFLEET) at RAF Uxbridge,
north-west of London;
Royal Marines Commandos, Lympstone;
Flag Officer Plymouth at Torpoint (HMS *Raleigh*);
Flag Officer Scotland & Northern Ireland at Rosyth;
Britannia Royal Naval College at Dartmouth;
The latter may be disbanded in 1987/88.

Musicians are trained at Deal but are not Commando trained, operating a war role of medical aid and stretcher-bearer support to the Commando Forces. In 1987, it is said that a successful campaign was waged by the Royal Marines to prevent a single service music school being developed.

Band Service officers are commissioned from the ranks of the band service and it is not a specialization open to direct entry. Recruits have a wide range of musical instruments to play.

SPECIAL ATTACHED UNITS

Supporting the Royal Marines elements of Commando Forces and British amphibious operations are two very important attached units from the British Army. Because of its size, the Corps cannot provide adequate manpower nor funding for artillery support and the many roles of combat engineers, so to cover this the Royal Artillery and the Royal Engineers have specialist regiments dedicated to the Commando Forces order of battle.

29 COMMANDO LIGHT REGIMENT ROYAL ARTILLERY

British Army support for the Royal Marines includes a commando-trained artillery regiment which was the successor to a distinguished unit of Second World War fame. During the post-War reorganization of the British military, 25 Field Regiment, Royal Artillery was redesignated 29 Field Regiment for service in such 'hot spots' as Palestine, Egypt and Cyprus, before being based permanently at Plymouth's Royal Citadel.

Since 1961, when the then War Department agreed to a request to provide supporting artillery for the Royal Marines Commandos, the regiment has been closely associated with the Corps. After 29 Regiment was selected for the Commando-support task, it was regrouped into detached batteries for actions in Kuwait and Aden.

Commando training followed during January and February 1962 and the coveted 'green berets' were presented by the then Commandant General Royal Marines in May 1962. When conflict with rebels in Brunei and then Indonesia broke out, a battery was flown to Brunei to support commando operations with its 105 mm Pack Howitzers, and that was the first time that the Regiment had used its guns in anger. Later, elements of 29 Cdo Regt RA were to support Parachute Regiment operations in Bahrain and Aden and the Royal Marines in Hong Kong, Sarawak and Malaya.

148 (Meiktila) Cdo Forward Observation Post Battery based at RM Poole, Dorset is a battery without guns. The main role of the battery is to spot for naval gunfire support (NGS) by providing Commando-trained Naval Gunfire Forward Observation posts.

Part of a battery from 29 Commando Light Regiment Royal Artillery lands from a specialist British Army landing craft during exercises in Norway. The 105 mm Light Gun is pulled by the Volvo Bv 202E 'band wagon' (RM).

The battery co-operates in this work with various other operational arms, including the Special Boat Squadron, because much of the Battery's work would be behind enemy lines.

289 Commando Battery (Volunteers) is based at East Ham, London and has the distinction of being the only Territorial Army Bty to be under direct command of a regular regiment. Before 1982 the Battery's troops wore the red beret of the Parachute Regiment but since 1983, it is 'green beret' qualified.

Headquarters Battery, based at Plymouth's Royal Citadel provides the command and control, administration and other non-gunnery support to the other batteries.

Each of the operational gun batteries is equipped with six Royal Ordnance 105 mm Light Guns, with towing tractor, usually a 1½ tonnes Land Rover, and other support vehicles. Each battery's equipment is air transportable by Sea King HC 4 helicopter, as an underslung load.

Naval Gunfire Forward Observation (NGFO) spotting team consists of an officer, a bombardier, a lance bombardier, a naval communications rating and a driver/operator. To fulfil the various optical functions required, the team is trained in small boat insertion, parachuting and abseiling. In addition, for Advance Force Operations (behind enemy lines), two parties are diver trained to enable them to be inserted by submarine or other craft for a silent, almost undetectable operation alongside the Special Boat Squadron.

Every man in the 148 Cdo FO Bty has to be Commando and

parachute trained and must pass the pre-parachute selection course, known as P Company, at Aldershot. Every officer is a qualified Forward Air Controller and every soldier has successfully completed a 12-week Naval Gunfire Assistants (Basic) course which introduces him to all aspects of NGS, including the use of Morse code and other communications techniques.

After the basic course, soldiers are selected for the advanced course which includes completing the Signals Advanced course at Larkhill. Naturally every officer and soldier is physically fit and training is undertaken every day.

Teams are deployed away from RM Poole on a regular basis, including the work-up of the Caribbean Guardship in NGS when the hand-over is completed between the respective ships at Belize. Work is also undertaken with the Allied Command Europe Mobile Force (a multi-national NATO force) in Norway and Turkey, and superb support was given by the guns at the regiment during the Falklands campaign.

59 INDEPENDENT COMMANDO REGIMENT ROYAL ENGINEERS

Formed as 59 Field Company in 1900, 59 Ind Cdo Sqn RE provides engineer support for 3 Cdo Bde RM, being responsible for all engineer work within the Brigade area.

In Royal Marines and Commando Forces terms, this work

Assault engineers can be landed by raiding craft on remote shorelines, under the cover of darkness, to attack and destroy key enemy installations (RM/A1 Campbell).

includes booby–traps, mine laying and clearance, route main-tenance and denial, bridging, rafting, water supply, snow clearance and support to 29 Commando Light Regiment Royal Artillery. The Squadron is also responsible for setting up bulk fuel installations as part of the Beach Support Area (BSA) and for this purpose, as well as for the reconnaissance of beaches, the squadron maintains a full diving team. Included in the Squadron strength of 9 officers and 253 soldiers is a workshop from the Royal Electrical and Mechanical Engineers (REME).

The squadron has a history of support to Commando Forces, including the period 1968-71, when as 59 Field Squadron RE, the squadron was based in Singapore. The Squadron reformed at Plymouth in April 1971 and became an integral part of the Royal Marines Commando Forces. During the Falklands conflict, the Squadron provided engineer support to all Commando units. In doing so it fought in every major battle.

THE ROYAL MARINES
AND THE ROYAL NAVY

In the order of battle of the British armed forces, the Royal Marines has a special place, not just because of the Corps's elite status, professional standing and ability, but also because of the unique position it occupies. The Royal Marines are soldiers with many of the traditions, practices and equipment of the British Army, but also belonging to the Royal Navy's chain of command.

The key role played by the fighting arm of the service, 3 Commando Royal Marines, in the NATO defence plans of northern Norway and other locations is directly supported by the Royal Navy's Air Commando Squadrons. These helicopter squadrons are not to be confused with the Brigade's own air squadron of Gazelle and Lynx helicopters, but are co-located support helicopters.

The operational concept for the air commando support dates back to the world's first successful amphibious helicopter assault during the 1956 Suez crisis when elements of the Commando forces were transported ashore by Whirlwind helicopters embarked in Light Fleet aircraft carriers. Later the operational doctrine was expanded for the Borneo operations during the Confrontation with Indonesia. Today, the Royal Navy and Royal Marines air support units work together in close-knit harmony.

To provide commando air support, especially in terms of logistical re-supply and troop movement, the Royal Navy's Fleet Air Arm provides two front-line helicopter units equipped with the Westland Sea King HC 4, the commando version of its medium antisubmarine warfare helicopter. In addition, there is an air commando training squadron, also equipped with the Sea King, which can be called into emergency front line service in wartime.

It was proved in the Falklands that the helicopter is a vital tool in a fluid and flexible war scenario, when men and material have to be moved rapidly across country but the relationship is deep-rooted in British post-war military doctrine.

Following the Suez operation, the Royal Navy embarked on a programme of converting the smaller aircraft carriers of the Light Fleet type into Commando Carriers equipped with facilities for troops, including the provision of landing craft and using the flight

The Royal Navy provides the major helicopter logistical lift for the Royal Marines with the Westland Sea King HC 4 support helicopter. The helicopter's cabin can accommodate the personal equipment which more than twenty marines would need to live in the mountains for a month (RN/Invincible/H.Amliwala).

deck to accommodate support helicopters rather than fixed-wing aircraft. The typical Commando Carriers, like *Albion* and *Bulwark*, were capable of carrying the 900 men of a Commando group (riflemen, support equipment, artillery and engineers) and exercises proved it was possible to land them all during a two-hour operation if the weather was favourable.

In the 1960s, the active Commando Carrier was stationed in the Mediterranean area, providing support to such incidents as the 1961 Kuwait crisis and the Aden emergency, after a sea passage through the Suez Canal and Red Sea. Later the warship type, then *Hermes*, was present to evacuate British and Commonwealth citizens during the Turkish invasion of Cyprus.

After the withdrawal from the Far East in the early 1970s, the Commando Carriers were used to support the British commitment to NATO by transporting Royal Marines to exercises in Norway, Canada and the West Indies. The Commando Carriers were later joined by the Assault Ships – Landing Platforms Dock or LPD to

After disembarking troops and their equipment on the snow, the Sea King lifts away for another load. The marines huddle over the equipment to prevent the helicopter's downwash from blowing it away (Patrick Allen).

NATO – and later in the decade to be supported by ro-ro (roll-on, roll-off) ferries as defence cuts brought about the end of the Commando Carrier –the Landing Platform Helicopter or LPH.

After *Bulwark* was paid off in 1981 and *Hermes* completed her last exercise in 1983, the Commando embarkation role, albeit a secondary one to the type, has been carried out by the 'Invincible' Class light aircraft carriers. It is now thought that no opposed assaults will be mounted in European waters and so the role envisaged for the aircraft carriers is to provide a means of transporting Commando forces prior to war breaking out and to the carriers being diverted to their primary role of anti-submarine warfare.

During the Falklands campaign in 1982, it was proved that the Royal Marines could be carried into action, albeit a limited, undeclared war, by the use of Ships Taken Up From Trade (STUFT) such as the SS *Canberra* and the RMS *Queen Elizabeth 2*. Such ships could not be expected to be used in a 'hot' war against the current NATO potential enemy of the Warsaw Pact.

This change of afloat support for the Royal Marines has meant a change of operational role for the support helicopters. In 1986, the last Wessex HU 5 transport helicopter was replaced in front line service by the more powerful Sea King. For ship-to-ship transfer prior to landing, the Sea King now provides a rapid means of moving equipment as it can lift 3.4 tonnes (7,500 lb) underslung for short transits or 2.7 tonnes (6,000 lb) for longer sorties. These loads could include the 1 tonne Land Rover and trailer, or the 105 mm light gun and ammunition. Internally, 25 fully armed and equipped mountain warfare troops can be carried over a distance of 65 nm (120 km) and a smaller group for a further radius of action.

Following the Falklands experience, future equipment for the Sea King includes self-defence missiles or countermeasures and a continued improvement of the helicopter's night flying capability. During the Falklands conflict, some helicopters and specially-trained crews from 846 Naval Air Squadron were able to land troops and special forces parties behind enemy lines under cover of darkness because the pilots and aircrewmen wore passive night vision goggles. Later generation night vision goggles and specially modified cockpit lighting is now available for the operational role in Norway.

Norway will be a critical area of Royal Marines/Royal Navy co-operation because of the limited surface transport routes and in winter because of the weather conditions which will make any movement on the ground difficult. The helicopters and their crews train for three months of the year in Norway every winter to maintain a state of readiness which can ensure helicopter support for the Royal Marines.

Not only men but also vehicles can be moved by helicopter, as this Sea King demonstrates by lifting a Land Rover from HMS Invincible's flight deck (RN).

ROYAL NAVY SUPPORT HELICOPTERS WESTLAND SEA KING HC 4

Purpose *Air Commando;* **Crew** *1/2 pilots; 1 aircrewman; 28 armed troops;* **Squadrons** *707; 845; 846;* **Range** *664 nm (1,230 km);* **Ferry range** *814 nm (1,507 km);* **Endurance** *5.9 hours;* **Max speed** *Circa 125 knots (232 km/h);* **Cruise speed** *112 knots (208 km/h);* **Service ceiling** *1,525 m;* **Rate of climb** *616 m/min;* **Length** *17.02 m; 22.15 m (rotors);* **Height** *5.13 m;* **Cabin height** *1.9 m;* **Width** *18.9 m (rotors turning);* **Rotor diameter** *18.9 m (main); 3.15 m (tail);* **Main door size** *1.72 m x 1.52 m;* **Personnel door** *0.92 m x 1.67 m;* **Weapons** *GPMG (door-mounted);* **Engine** *2 x RR Gnome turboshafts rated at 1,660 shp;* **Fuel capacity** *3,636 litres;* **All-up weight** *9,525 kg;* **Basic aircraft** *5,070 kg;* **Embarked** *Shore-based (can operate from any amphibious ship or RFA; during Falklands Deployment operated from* Canberra *and* Queen Elizabeth 2*).*

For the first time, the Royal Marines have a means of transporting their heavier equipment without needing the assistance of ASW Sea Kings. The Sea King HC 4 (known commercially as the Westland Commando) is the best heavy lift air commando aircraft and has become an outstanding troop transport even in the north of Norway during the winter months. Typically, the Sea King HC 4 can carry 28 fully armed men to action and de-plane them through the large cargo door, or it can carry their equipment internally or their vehicles as underslung loads (up to 3,600 kg). It has an all-weather day or night capability and automatic flight control systems for easy operation in the hover.

In the casevac role, the aircraft can carry a total of 16 injured with their medical attendant over a distance of 610 km or 329 nm at sea level.

In the RN, the Sea King HC 4 operates in the field alongside the Royal Marines but it can be embarked for short periods in the CVSs or one of the Assault Landing Ships (LPDs).

The Sea King HC 4 (ordered following the cancellation of an ASW order from a foreign navy) first flew on September 26 1979. Since then it has been operational in the Falklands (including special operations using ANVIS night vision goggles) and Lebanon during the evacuation of British and Commonwealth subjects in 1984. Training roles have taken the helicopters to Europe and North America, with the annual winter training exercises in Norway. By 1986, 24 were in service (with nine more on order for delivery in 1987).

In late 1986, 845, the final front-line Wessex HU 5 squadron converted to the Sea King HC 4. A possible replacement by 2005 is the utility version of the EH 101, an Anglo-Italian helicopter which first flew in October 1987.

WESSEX HU 5

Purpose *Air Commando; logistic support; helo delivery;* **Crew** *1/2 pilots; 1 air-crewman; 16 troops* **Squadrons** *771; 772;* **Range** *270 nm (500 km);* **Endurance** *2.25 hours;* **Max speed** *132 knots (245 km/h);* **Cruise speed** *121 knots (225 km/h);* **Service ceiling** *1,676 m;* **Rate of climb** *500 m/min;* **Length** *14.74 m;* **Height** *4.93 m;* **Width** *3.7 m;* **Rotor diameter** *17.07 m;* **Weapons** *GPMG; Nord AS 11 ASM; 2.75-in/70 mm rocket launchers; flares;* **Engine** *2 x RR Gnome turboshafts;* **Fuel capacity** *Classified;* **All-up weight** *6,120 kg;* **Embarked** *Assault ships; CVSs; RFAs; LSLs; SAR Flights.*

Although the Wessex airframe has been around for a long time, it was only in 1963 that the first RN squadrons were equipped with the twin engined (1,350 shp) Wessex HU 5 for the Commando assault and logistical support role, mainly from the newly developed Commando Carriers. By the end of 1986, 845 Squadron had converted to the Sea King, which meant the phasing out of the Wessex HU 5 from commando service. Until 1988 the Wessex helicopter continued to fulfil a need for a helicopter to support the Royal Auxiliary Service, Flag Officer Sea Training and for SAR duties. The last unit, 772 Naval Air Squadron paid off on 31 March 1988.

Although now out of front-line service, the Westland Wessex HU 5 could still be used to transport troops and equipment in an emergency. This helicopter is pictured refuelling on the flight deck of HMS Fearless — note the empty LCVP davits forward of the flight deck.

ROYAL MARINES EQUIPMENT

PERSONAL WEAPONS
9 MM PISTOL AUTOMATIC L9A1

Calibre 9 *mm*; **Length** 0.196 *m*; **Length of barrel** 0.112 *m*; **Weight empty** 0.88 *kg*; **Weight loaded** 1.01 *kg*; **Muzzle velocity** 354 *m/s*; **Magazine capacity** 13 *rounds*; **Rate of fire** *Single-shot*; **Maximum effective range** 40–50 *m*.

This is the officer and special duties pattern pistol which has been standard since the 1940s. It is also known as the Browning 9 mm. The pistol is worn on the hip in a canvas holster or in a shoulder holster for special duties. It has an unusually large magazine capacity and can be used accurately by relative newcomers because of the long grip which can help steady the user's arm. The butt is also a fine combat weapon in its own right.

9 MM SUB-MACHINE GUN (SMG) L2A3

Calibre 9 *mm*; **Length (butt folded)** 0.482 *m*; **Length (butt extended)** 0.69 *m*; **Length of barrel** 0.198 *m*; **Weight empty** 2.7 *kg*; **Weight loaded** 3.5 *kg*; **Muzzle velocity** 390 *m/s*; **Magazine capacity** 34 *rounds*; **Rate of fire (cyclic)** 550 *rpm*; **Rate of fire (practical)** 102 *rpm*; **Rate of fire (single-shot)** 40 *rpm*; **Maximum effective range** 200 *m*.

The standard issue Browning 9 mm pistol, its holster, magazine and cleaning equipment (RM).

This is the universally known Sterling SMG which is the replacement of the equally well known Sten gun of the Second World War. It is the third modification on the standard 1945 pattern Sterling and is used by support units and for house clearing and associated work. It is possible to fit a bayonet to the muzzle. In service, many users tape two magazines together for quick changes.

7.62 MM SELF-LOADING RIFLE (SLR) L1A2

Calibre 7.62 mm; **Length overall** 1.143 m; **Length of barrel** 0.5334 m; **Weight empty** 4.337 kg; **Weight loaded (20-round magazine)** 5.074 kg; **Muzzle velocity** 838 m/s; **Magazine capacity** 20 or 30 rounds; **Rate of fire** 40 rpm; **Maximum effective range** 600 m plus.

The NATO standard rifle, known as the FN, SLR or FAL in various formations. The 7.62 mm gun is equipped to fire ball rounds (L2A2 or L11A1); it has fittings for a bayonet (L1A1 or L1A4); for 0.22-in conversion in order to facilitate indoor range work (L12A1); for a grenade launcher (L1A2) which is rarely used by the RM; for the Infantry Weapon Sight (IWS) type L1A1 or L1A2 and for the blank

Until recently, the SLR (Self-Loading Rifle) was the standard infantry weapon of the British forces. Today, very few regular Royal Marines and some of the Royal Marines Reserve units are still issued with the weapon. The picture shows the rifle, bayonet and scabbard, magazine and sling (RM).

firing attachment L6A1 (with yellow cap on muzzle). The basic sight is most commonly used but in certain places the Sight Unit Infantry Trilux (SUIT or L1A1/L1A2) is fitted; this looks for all intents and purposes like the back half of a telescopic sight, as seen in American war films.

SUIT Specification: **Weight** 340 g; **Length** 188 mm;,**Height** 69 mm; **Field of view** 8°; **Sight settings** 300 and 500 m; **Magnification** x 4. The SLR is now fitted with plastic furniture and the butt may be varied in length by using one of four different butt-plates, thus enabling the weapon to be adjusted to suit the stature of the individual firer.

5.56 MM INDIVIDUAL WEAPON (SA 80)

Calibre 5.56 mm; **Length overall** 0.77 mm; **Weight loaded** 4.28 kg; **Muzzle velocity** 900 m/s; **Magazine capacity** 20 or 30 rounds; **Rate of fire** 700 rpm; **Combat range** 400 m.

Known orginally as the XL70E3, the SA 80 (Small Arm for the

Commandos of 45 Cdo Grp RM exercise in Norway with the SA80 self-loading rifle (furthest from the camera) and the Light Support Weapon from the same Royal Ordnance design. Both marines are wearing the new lightweight combat helmet (RM).

1980s) entered Royal Marines service in 1986 and was first seen during the Buckingham Palace Guard duties performed by the Royal Marines that summer. Replacement of the SLR with this weapon will continue into the 1990s, but already trials have been successfully carried out in Borneo, Norway and Belize.

SA 80 has the advantage of being smaller than the existing SLR and is therefore said to be easier to handle, especially during helicoper, landing craft and small craft work. It is the standard weapon for the British Army and other services, using the NATO standard 5.56 mm round.

7.62 MM SNIPER RIFLE L42A1

Calibre 7.62 *mm*; **Length** 1.181 *m*; **Length of barrel** 0.699 *m*; **Weight empty** 4.43 *kg*; **Weight loaded** *Classified*; **Muzzle velocity** 838 *m/s*; **Magazine capacity** 10 *rounds*; **Rate of fire** *Single-shot only*; **Maximum effective range** 1,200 *m*.

This is a classic sniper rifle which would be used in many battle areas to pick off special targets, such as enemy commanders. It is the result of re-barrelling the old Lee Enfield Service Rifle and is most often seen with a telescopic sight, known as Sighting Telescope (L1A1). The sniping role is difficult and dangerous; various types of ammunition are used as well as several types of grip and sling. Replacement by the **Accuracy International Model PM** is thought to be underway at troop level.

5.56 MM AR-15/M16 RIFLE

Calibre 5.56 *mm*; **Length** 0.99 *m*; **Length of barrel** 0.508 *m*; **Weight (gun alone)** 3.1 *kg*; **Weight loaded (20-round magazine)** 3.68 *kg*; **Weight loaded (30-round magazine)** 3.82 *kg*; **Muzzle velocity** 1,000 *m/s*; **Magazine capacity** 20 *or* 30 *rounds*; **Rate of fire (cyclic)** 700-960 *rpm*; **Rate of fire (practical)** 40-60 *rpm*; **Maximum effective range** 400 *m*.

The Armalite (or M16 or AR-15) is a small calibre assault rifle used in the British Armed forces primarily for close-quarter and jungle warfare and it was in this role that the RM first became familiar with it. It is now used by the Corps for special operations (SBS) and by reconnaissance troops. It is well liked by those who operate it, although there is some conjecture about the light weight of the projectile as compared to the SLR. It is a good close-quarters weapon

The US-pattern Armalite M-16 rifle, known as the AR-15 to the Royal Marines. The picture shows the rifle, its bayonet and sling attached, and three of the 5.56 mm rounds. This is a jungle fighting and special operations weapon (RM).

and has what will most probably be chosen as the calibre for future NATO personal weapons— 5.56 mm.

7.62 MM LIGHT MACHINE-GUN L4A4

Calibre 7.62 mm; **Length** 1.133 m; **Length of barrel** 0.536 m; **Weight empty** 9.96 kg; **Weight loaded** 10.68 kg; **Muzzle velocity** 869 m/s; **Magazine capacity** 30 rounds*; **Rate of fire (cyclic)** 500-575 rpm; **Rate of fire (practical)** 120 rpm; **Rate of fire (single-shot)** 40 rpm; **Maximum effective range** 800 m.

This is the Light Machine-Gun (LMG) which the Corps use mainly in the jungle and Arctic for light anti-aircraft and anti-personnel operations. It is basically a modified Bren Gun of Second World War vintage which was replaced at Section level by the GPMG (General Purpose Machine–Gun) in the 1960s.

At a Command Post in Norway, Mne David Robinson mans the Light Machine-Gun whilst Gunnery Sergeant Victor Elliott, an USMC exchange senior NCO with 3 Cdo Bde, looks on.

The standard support weapon has been the General Purpose Machine-Gun until the advent of the Light Support weapon which is still entering service. This GPMG is manned by marines from City of London RMR.

7.62 MM GENERAL PURPOSE MACHINE-GUN (GPMG) L7A2

Calibre 7.62 mm; **Length as LMG** 1.232 m; **Length as HMG** 1.049 m; **Length of barrel** 0.629 m; **Weight empty (LMG role)** 10.9 kg; **Weight loaded (LMG role)** 13.85 kg; **Weight of tripod** 13.64 kg; **Muzzle velocity** 838 m/s; **Type of feed** 100-round belt; **Rate of fire (cyclic)** 625-750 rpm; **Rate of fire (LMG role)** 100 rpm; **Rate of fire (HMG role)** 200 rpm; **Maximum effective range (LMG)** 800 m; **Maximum effective range (HMG)** 1,800 m.

The L7A2 GPMG is based on the FN MAG and is used by the RM as a Section weapon in all areas of operation. It is particularly valuable as a sustained fire machine-gun (GPMG SF) when it is fitted with a tripod mount. It is fully automatic, belt-fed, gas-operated, air-cooled and can continue firing for considerable periods. The gun is fed from left to right using M13-type disintegrating linked belts. There is a gas regulator and a flash-hider attachment to aid concealment.

The GPMG SF is designed to give sustained fire for effective infantry cover and control, day or night, on a range of predetermined targets. The SF kit is easily portable and can quickly be in action. It is normal to have at least two marines at the SF location—the aimer/firer and the loader; in addition, whenever possible, a third man acts as a gun controller. Spare barrels are necessary in this role.

SF kit specification: **Overall folded dimensions** 190 x 190 x 810 mm; **Weight** 13.4 kg; **Traverse** 360°; **Elevation** −11° to +22°; **Tripod type** L4A1; **Sight for SF role** Sight Unit C2; **Magnification** 1.7.

5.56 MM LIGHT SUPPORT WEAPON

Calibre 5.56 *mm*; **Length overall** 0.9 *m*; **Weight loaded** 4.88 *kg*; **Muzzle velocity** 945 *m/s*; **Rate of fire** 700/850 *rpm*; **Combat range** 1,000 *m*.

This bi-pod, mounted, light support machine gun first entered service with the Corps in 1986, and will replace the standard 7.62 mm GPMG in Royal Marines service. Replacement will be on a unit basis and continue until 1991, although a number of specialist tasks will still require the retention of the GPMG well into the next decade.

The Light Support Weapon is completely compatible with the SA 80 and again uses the NATO standard 5.56 mm round.

7.62 MM COMPETITION RIFLE L39A1

Calibre 7.62 *mm*; **Length** 1.18 *m*; **Length of barrel** 0.7 *m*; **Weight empty** 4.42 *kg*; **Weight loaded** *Circa* 5 *kg*; **Muzzle velocity** 841 *m/s*; **Magazine capacity** 10 *rounds*; **Rate of fire** *Single shot only*; **Maximum effective range** 1,000 *m plus*.

Used in place of the SLR for competition work, this is a bolt-action rifle using the green spot target ammunition (L2A2) for training and actual eventing. Bisley in Surrey is the main venue for such shoots.

The Light Support Weapon began to supplement and replace the GPMG in 1987 and by 1990 will be used by all formations within the Corps (RM).

51 MM LIGHT MORTAR

Calibre 50.8 *mm*; **Length of barrel overall** 0.7 *m*; **Length of bore** 0.515 *m*; **Weight of barrel** 1.5 *kg*; **Weight of breech piece** 0.99 *kg*; **Weight of sight unit** 0.65 *kg*; **Weight of monopod** 0.48 *kg*; **Weight of base plate** 0.76 *kg*; **Weight complete in action** 4.6 *kg*; **Maximum range** 800 *m*; **Minimum range** 150 *m*; **Bomb weight (HE L1A1)** 0.68 *kg*; **Bomb weight (smoke L1A1)** 0.68 *kg*; **Bomb weight (illuminating L1A3)** 0.85 *kg*; **Rate of fire (maximum)** 8 *rpm for 2 minutes*; **Rate of fire (normal)** 3 *rpm for 5 minutes*.

This is a man-portable light mortar which is rapidly replacing the old 2-in muzzle-loading mortar at troop level. The latter is still found in RMR use at CTC, however, so a specification is given: **Calibre 51.2 mm/2 in**; **Length complete** 0.482 m; **Weight complete** 3.3 kg; **Maximum range** 500 m; **Bomb weight (smoke)** 0.909 kg; **Bomb weight (signal)** 0.511 kg.

The 51 mm is designed to: provide rapid and accurate smoke screen up to 750 m from the mortar; bring down quick, accurate and lethal neutralizing or protective fire on the section front; provide target illumination for 'Charlie G', MAW and Milan AT systems; be capable of direct or indirect fire with only one man; and to overlap in range with the 81 mm mortar.

The 51 mm has increased range, lethality and accuracy over the old 2-in mortar, but the latter's ammunition can be used if required.

This mortar will fire explosive, smoke and illuminating bombs which have an aluminium casing and are fitted with plastic rings to prevent damage to the barrel. There are also drill and practice rounds.

Round	Weight	Filling	Remarks
HE	1.025 kg	TNT	272 mm long with fragmentation effect
Smoke	0.95 kg	HCE	Time delay of six seconds, duration 120 seconds
Illuminating	0.825 kg	Various	Maximum range to light-up 750 m; burst height 250 m; duration 70 seconds.

A rate of fire of three rounds per minute for five minutes (15 rounds) can be achieved, but it is more usual to require eight

Above *Sentry duty. A Royal Marine Commando from 40 Commando during a temperate climate exercise on the Otterburn Ranges near Newcastle-upon-Tyne in 1986 (PO(Phot) Alistair Campbell).*

Below *The modern Royal Marine is now equipped with the Royal Ordnance SA80 infantry weapon and the 'plastic' helmet. Further improvements will include the new webbing pack to carry the 'bergen' or haversack (PO(Phot) Alistair Campbell).*

Above left *Although Arctic Norway has become the traditional theatre of operation for the Royal Marines, commando elements train in other climes. In 1985-86, men from 40 Cdo RM were sent to Belize in Central America for jungle training (PO(Phot) Alistair Campbell).*

Left *Sergeant Scott of 40 Cdo RM stands guard over one of the RAF Harrier GR 3 close air support and air defence aircraft based in Belize (PO (Phot) Alistair Campbell).*

Above *In the deserts of Arabia, the Royal Marines were active during Exercise Saif Saree in November/December 1986 and are photographed here operating with Sea King HC4 helicopters of 846 Naval Air Squadron (PO(Phot) Alistair Campbell).*

Right *Northern Ireland has also been a trouble-spot frequented by the Corps. During a tour in South Armagh in 1983, men of 40 Cdo RM protected firemen from the Provisional IRA at a timber yard fire in Newry (PO(Phot) Alistair Campbell).*

Above Into the sunset. A patrol of four Royal Marines, armed, trained and equipped to be self-sufficient for days at a time, sets out towards the objective (Cdo Forces News Team).

Below Exercise Bold Guard, Norway, in 1986 provided the Corps with training in counter-insurgency and against imagined Spetsnaz incursions. Here a 'suspect' is taken away for interrogation (PO(Phot) Alistair Campbell).

rounds per minute for two minutes in most tactical situations. The mortar is manufactured by the Royal Ordnance Factory.

66 MM ROCKET HEAT L1A1

Calibre *66 mm;* **Length extended** *0.893 m;* **Length closed** *0.655 m;* **Length of rocket** *0.508 m;* **Weight complete** *2.37 kg;* **Weight of rocket** *1 kg;* **Muzzle velocity** *145 m/s;* **Maximum effective range** *300 m;* **Armour penetration** *Up to 270 mm steel plate.*

This is the American M72 HEAT (High Explosive Anti-Tank) weapon to give anti-tank protection at Section level. Basically it is a man-portable, disposable system which can be used against most modern AFVs. This weapon is in service with Commandos and RMR units but is currently being replaced by the MAW. It is essentially an extendable tube with primitive sight.

81 MM MORTAR L16A1

Calibre *81 mm;* **Length of barrel overall** *1.27 m;* **Weight of barrel** *12.27 kg;* **Weight of mounting** *11.8 kg;* **Weight of sight unit** *3.40 kg;* **Weight of base plate** *11.6 kg;* **Weight complete in action** *39.6 kg;* **Muzzle velocity (maximum)** *255 m/s;* **Maximum range** *5,660 m;* **Maximum range (HE L31E3)** *5,800 m plus;* **Minimum range** *180 m;* **Elevation** *45° to 80°;* **Traverse** *5° left/ right at 45°;* **Bomb weight (HE L15A3)** *4.47 kg;* **Bomb weight (Smoke L19A4)** *4.49 kg;* **Rate of fire** *12 rpm.*

An 81 mm mortar team wades ashore during a Mediterranean Sea exercise. Besides the mortar, broken down for the three marines to carry, each man is armed with the Stirling SMG (RM).

Although of medium calibre, this mortar is considered to be a lightweight type. It is accurate, portable and reliable with an extensive range of ammunition available. It is equivalent to a medium artillery piece in some roles using a bipod mount. There are usually six in a Mortar Troop.

The main feature of this weapon is its high accuracy, being 0.5 per cent in any range setting. It is broken down into a three-man load with the heaviest part, the barrel, weighing 12.28 kg. It is also capable of a high sustained rate of fire.

The ammunition is specially made and HE, WP and illumination rounds are available to match the mortar's own considerable characteristics. Three basic rounds are British-made—HE, WP and practice (the illumination round for the 81 mm is under development at present). HE round (L15A3): **Weight** 4.45 kg; **Filling** TNT/RDX: **Overall length** 0.472 m; **Range** 180–5,660 m. Smoke (L19A4); **Weight** 4.45 kg; **Filling** White phosphorus (willie peter); **Overall length** 0.46 m; **Range** As HE. Practice (L21): A re-usable round with a range of 25–75 m.

84 MM CARL GUSTAV L14A1

Calibre *84 mm;* **Length of barrel** *1.13 m;* **Weight complete** *16 kg;* **Muzzle velocity** *160 m/s;* **Weight of HEAT round L40A4** *2.59 kg;* **Weight of HEAT projectile** *1.7 kg;* **Range, anti-tank (mobile)** *400 m;* **Range, anti-tank (stationary)** *500 m;* **Range, HE and smoke** *1,000 m;* **Rate of fire** *6 rpm;* **Armour penetration (HEAT at 60°)** *228 mm.*

Company level anti-tank defences include the 84 mm Carl Gustav which is credited with the disabling of an Argentine corvette during the attack on South Georgia in 1982. Mne Mark Crozier of Z Coy, 45 Cdo Gp, poses with the weapon at a command post.

This is the Swedish-made 'Charlie G' which is the largest weapon at troop level. It will be replaced after 1988 by the LAW 80. It is designed as an anti-tank weapon which is shoulder-held in action; it is recoilless and capable of knocking out any known tank. There is a kit available to convert it for training purposes to 6.5 mm; other rounds are HEAT (L40A4) (weight 2.59 kg) and Smoke.

LIGHT ANTI-ARMOUR WEAPON 80

Projectile calibre 94 mm; **Launcher length extended** 1.5 m; **Weight overall** 9.5 kg; **Weight of projectile** 4 kg; **Maximum range** 500 m; **Combat range** 300 m.

Left *The latest man-held anti-tank weapon for the British armed forces is the Hunting Engineering LAW 90 which is now entering service with the Royal Marines (Hunting).*

Below *The basic components of the LAW 90 include the launching tube, missile and firing mechanism (Hunting).*

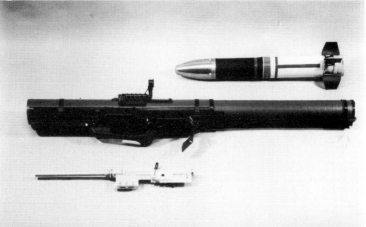

Formally called LAW, the Hunting Engineering light anti-armour system is designed for defence against modern main battle tanks and other armoured vehicles. It has an integral spotting rifle to give high kill probability and the operator requires minimal training. Service introduction is expected by 1988.

MILAN

Weight of missile 6.65 *kg;* **Weight of missile and container** 11.5 *kg;* **Weight of launch unit** 15.5 *kg;* **Length of missile** 0.769 m; **Body diameter (minimum)** 90 *mm;* **Span** 0.225 m; **Weight of warhead** 2.98 *kg;* **Weight of warhead charge** 1.45 *kg;* **Velocity** 75 to 200 *m/s;* **Maximum range** 2,000 m; **Minimum range** 25 m; **Rate of fire (maximum range)** 3–4 *rpm;* **Time of flight to 2,000 m** *Up to 13 seconds;* **Armour penetration** *Up to 352 mm.*

The Milan *(Missile d'Infantrie Léger Anti-Char)* is a second generation wire-guided ATM which replaced the Aérospatiale SS 11 in French Army service. It was ordered for the British Armed Forces in 1978 and is manufactured under licence by British Aerospace. The standard Milan team is one man with the support of one or two with extra missiles, and in the RM the weapon equips the Anti-Tank Troop of a Support Company within a Commando. The usual complement of a Troop is one officer, 48 Marines and 14 launchers, plus

The multi-national Euromissile Milan provides medium-range defence against armoured vehicles, and in the Falklands was proved to be capable of destroying hardened sangars and gun positions (RM).

Dug in to a gun pit on Salisbury Plain, a Milan unit prepares to engage enemy armour. The firing post and missiles are easily transported by the firing team in a Land Rover, by helicopter or landing craft.

nine vehicles for transportation. The usefulness of Milan depends on how mobile the team is because, once spotted, the Milan emplacement or position is bound to come under attack, such is the effectiveness of the weapon. Armour penetration is 352 mm.

The system comprises a launcher on a tripod support with clip missiles in sealed containers. The missile is fin-stabilized and powered by a rocket motor which ignites away from the launcher. Milan has replaced the Wombat recoilless gun.

BLOWPIPE

Weight complete *19.39 kg;* **Weight with IFF** *21.2 kg;* **Length of missile** *1.349 m;* **Body diameter** *76.2 mm;* **Span** *0.274 m;* **Maximum range** *3,000 m plus.*

This is a lightweight anti-aircraft missile which equips the Air Defence Troop of a Commando Brigade Headquarters for immediate area defence against low-flying aircraft and assault helicopters. Normally about a dozen missile launchers are available. Like Milan, Blowpipe is supplied in a sealed container for fitting to the launcher tube. The missile is powered by two rocket motors and is aimed with a monocular sight. The warhead is fitted for proximity

Since the 1970s there has been an increasing threat from fixed-wing aircraft and armed helicopters. One of the first missile systems developed to counter the threat was the Shorts Blowpipe, seen here in the hands of an Air Defence Troop marine (RM).

or impact detonation and an IFF unit can be used to establish whether an aircraft is hostile or not. In the field, there would not be time for visual identification of a small, fast moving and low flying target. It is thought that the Blowpipe missile's radio guidance instructions cannot be jammed, because of the short range involved. The system proved to be very effective in bridgehead and landing ground defence during the Falklands campaign and it accounted for several enemy aircraft.

JAVELIN

Weight (missile) *11 kg;* **Maximum range** *4,000 m;* other details as Blowpipe.

Blowpipe is being superceded in RM service by the more advanced Javelin system which is also equipping the ships' detachments of the Armilla Patrol (Shorts).

This new portable air defence missile system is a development of Blowpipe introduced into Royal Marines service to meeting the evolving requirements of ground force defence (particularly as an effective stand-off range system against helicopter attacks). Deliveries began in 1986.

In 1987, it was announced that detachments of Royal Marines were embarked in the destroyers and frigates of the Armilla Patrol, armed with Javelin shoulder-launched missiles to strengthen the close-in anti-missile and air defences of the warships.

SPECIALIST EQUIPMENT

Although the Mountain and Arctic Warfare (M&AW) cadres have special weapons for their environment, and it is presumed that the Special Boat Squadron (SBS) would be similarly equipped with whatever equipment was thought necessary, the RM has very little special equipment. The major exception to this is in Northern Ireland where the bulk used is of British Army origin: Nightsun illumination for use in Lynx and Gazelle helicopters; Skyshout speakers for use in Gazelle helicopters; Pocketscope hand-held night vision aids (also found in Hong Kong); and Claribel 2B2981 (GS No 14 Mk 1) and Prowler surveillance radar. These items are described in the *Encyclopaedia of the Modern British Army*.

A patrol from 45 Cdo Gp shows the variety of weapons in service and the use of nuclear-biological-chemical warfare clothing, including the standard service Avon S10 respirator. From the left, the weapons are an SLR, using the crossed ski poles as a gun rest, an SLR being aimed from the prone position and an SMG being aimed from the kneel (RM).

Specialist equipment in Northern Ireland includes the internal security duty flak-jacket for body protection and, on the head, the riot helmet and visor (RM).

Several night vision aids are in more regular use, including the Individual Weapon Sight (IWS) L1A2 and the Telescope Straight II (L1E1); also known as 'Twiggy'. In Northern Ireland, it is usual for SLRs to be fitted with SUIT for clearer vision. RM Surveillance Troops are often equipped with the Night Observation Device (NOD). The IWS has a magnification of x 3.75, a 180-mil field of view and weighs 2.78 kg; 'Twiggy' a x 5.0 magnification, 129-mil field of view and weight of 11.0 kg. Details of the NOD are still classified.

MINES AND DETECTORS

There are a large number of mines available in the modern world and they have become a favourite weapon of terrorist groups, even though it is never possible to predict who will be killed or maimed as a result of detonation. More often than not in these cases it is the innocent civilian who is hurt. On the battlefield the mine can be used as an offensive or defensive weapon depending on tactics. It is not known whether mines are particularly effective in snow conditions.

CLAYMORE ANTI-PERSONNEL MINE M18A1

Weight *1.58 kg*; **Length** *0.216 m*; **Height** *0.083 m*; **Width** *0.035 m*; **Weight of charge** *0.68 kg*; **Range** *50 m (16 m rearwards)*.

This is an American-made device which is used to disrupt enemy patrols. It is a curved box with 700 'nasty' steel balls which are propelled by the explosive charge to a height of 1 m and a range of 50 m. Detonation is by remote control or trip wire. The device is carried in a bandolier.

HORIZONTAL ACTION ANTI-TANK MINE

Weight *12 kg*; **Length** *0.26 m*; **Diameter** *0.2 m*; **Range** *80 m*.

This French-made device is used against heavy vehicles such as armoured personnel carriers (APCs) and AFVs. It is located, in similar fashion to Claymore, at the side of a route used by vehicles and is exploded to cause as much damage to the tracks and softer parts as possible. The charge is propelled against the AFV/APC and can penetrate 70 mm of armour.

ANTI-TANK MINE Mk 7

Weight *13.6 kg*; **Diameter** *0.325 m*; **Height** *0.13 m*; **Weight of charge** *8.89 kg*.

The old Anti-Tank Mine Mk 7 is occasionally used for the RM for setting defensive minefields; it is more commonly used by the Army and is being replaced by a new Bar Mine Layer which will not see RM service at present.

MINE DETECTOR No 4C

Weight in use *9.15 kg*; **Weight in transit box** *14.4 kg*; **Search head length** *0.286 m*; **Search head height** *0.108 m*; **Search head width** *0.184 m*; **Amplifier depth** *0.216 m*; **Amplifier height** *0.108 m*; **Amplifier width** *0.108 m*; **Handle extended** *0.127 m*; **Handle collapsed** *0.38 m*; **Detection depth (soil)** *0.51 m*; **Detection depth (pavé)** *0.305 m*.

Left Mine warfare on land continues to present a threat to marching or riding troops. The Royal Marines use a series of special mine detectors (Cdo Forces New Team).

Right Amongst the latest systems of explosive detection being tested by the British forces is the Ai Security's Model 97 detector, especially useful for vehicle check points.

This is the standard metal mine detector used by the RM for sweeping paths and other areas where enemy mines may be located, and has been in service since 1968.

It is possible to use this device whilst walking or, if in action, in the prone position, because the handle and search head are adjustable to the conditions. Various anti-sweep devices such as iron filings can be overcome using the special selector for *pavé* material. Like all detectors of this type, it works on the principle of electromagnetic induction when two coils are in balance; any metallic object coming into the field is usually strong enough to put the balance out and so register.

P6/2 SWEEP METAL DETECTOR

Weight complete 4.5 kg; **Length of long probe** 1.016 m; **Length of short probe** 0.4 m; **Length of open loop probe** 1.143 m; **Length of personnel probe** 0.4 m; **Dimensions of electronic unit** 0.25 x 0.08 x 0.25 m.

The P6/2 Sweep metal and mine detector is a militarized version of the Plessey P6 pulse indication metal detector. In military use the Sweep is issued with four different probes which can be used to fulfil almost any detection role from conventional mine detection to personnel body searches. The probes are an open loop probe for normal ground searches, a ferrite rod for searching foliage and water locations, a short probe and the personnel search probe. Using the ferrite probe an object the size of an automatic pistol can be detected up to 0.28 metres away.

GRENADES

The grenades used by the RM are identical to the British Army pattern, and are covered in the companion volume, but are subject to review at present. They can be divided into three types: HE (High Explosive), Smoke and Irritant.

Anti-personnel hand grenade (L2A1) *This grenade can be used as a hand-thrown weapon with a range of 19 m or as a rifle projectile; the RM has chosen not to use it with the latter. It has the following specification:* **Weight of explosive** *170 g TNT;* **Length** *77.5 m. It is based on the American M26 series and there are two training grenades available for inert practice—L3A1 and L4A1. This is the standard RM hand grenade.*

Grenades are still a viable personal weapon; these smoke types are similar in physical structure to the high explosive and blast types used in combat situations.

SMOKE GENERATORS AND GRENADES

The RM's smoke grenades are due to change to the new XL6E1 and XL21E1 series currently under development during the next few years. These new designs will weigh about 0.5 kg, stand 140 mm high and have a diameter of 63.5 mm. Until they are in service the following grenades will continue to be used:

Type	Colours available	Weight	Height	Diameter
No 80	Red, yellow, blue, green	0.55 kg	140 mm	63.5 mm
No 83	Red, yellow, blue, green	0.5 kg	140 mm	63.5 mm
No 8*	White	1.75 kg	100 mm	100.0 mm
No 28†	White	2.5 kg	205 mm	100.0 mm

* Used as a training aid.
† Used to mark landing grounds and burns for 5 minutes.

Special smoke grenades include (from the left) No 80 smoke, L1A1 anti-riot irritant and the Mk 83 signal grenade. Signal grenades are available in red, green, yellow or blue and are used for communications between units or for ground-to-air marking; they last for up to 60 seconds (RM).

The 25 mm signal cartridge and the Very pistol are still used for dispensing smoke grenades for defence and rescue purposes. The cartridges are available in red, yellow, green and white single star and reach a height of 90 m with a burning time of six seconds. The pistol's designation is L4A2.

Thunderflash This is designed to give safe maximum simulation of battlefield conditions for training purposes.

AMMUNITION

Below are listed the current ammunition types for the standard 7.62 mm NATO guns; all rounds are 51 mm in length:

Designation	Description
Round 7.62 mm Ball L2A2	Normal service round for operational use
Round 7.62 mm Tracer L5A3	Tracer to 1,100 m; red colour
Round 7.62 mm Drill L1A2	Inert round for training purposes
Cartridge 7.62 mm Rifle Grenade L1A2	For projecting 'Super Energa' rifle grenade
Cartridge 7.62 mm Blank L13A1	Crimped blank for training use

IRRITANTS

Although these have mainly been used in Northern Ireland, there are two irritant grenades available to the Corps for IS and training purposes, both containing CS gas, which has become infamous in Ulster and elsewhere for crowd control. The RM use CS for NBC simulation and training.

Canister Irritants (L1A1/L2A1) are the major weapons, being only slightly different in their method of dispensing CS. The former (L1A1) is the older type which uses holes in the base and sides to emit gas, whereas the newer version has overcome the anti-canister measures of rioters by exploding to emit CS. Both canisters are 114 mm x 57 mm. Because they have proved ineffective they have been replaced by the **Hand Anti-Riot Irritant L13A1.** This is larger,

The signal pistol is used to fire smoke and anti-riot rounds, such as the L2A1 round pictured. The cartridge has a range of between 75 and 100 m, and lasts for 10 to 15 seconds (RM).

175 mm x 66 mm, weighs 0.55 kg and can be thrown about 25 m unaided.

Northern Ireland theatre

As the Royal Marines operate in the Province as an Army battalion, it uses the standard Army anti-riot and IS equipment, including Grenade discharger (L1A1); Anti-riot gas dischargers (L6A1, L9A1, L11A1); 1.5-in Anti-riot cartridges (L3A1) and Baton rounds—plastic and rubber bullets. These items are described fully in *Encyclopaedia of the Modern British Army* by Terry Gander, also published by Patrick Stephens.

ARTILLERY WEAPONS

In 1804, the British government authorized the formation of the Royal Marines artillery companies, later to be known as the Royal Marines Artillery. The RMA amalgamated with the Royal Marines Light Infantry in 1923 to form the Corps of Royal Marines. During the Second World War, there were several specialist units of Royal Marines, including the RM Armoured Support Goup which was equipped with the 95 mm Gun-Howitzer Centaur battle tank.

The first post-Second World War permanent attachment of artillery took place in 1961 with the formation of 29 Commando Light Regiment Royal Artillery which underwent amalgamation in 1976 (see page 79).

105 MM LIGHT GUN

This artillery weapon had replaced the long-serving Pack Howitzer in Commando Forces' service by the Falklands conflict in 1982. It is

Right *A 105 mm Light Gun from 79 (Kirkee) Cdo Bty RA in its camouflaged firing position.*

Below *Ready to be flown ashore, these 105 mm Light Guns are the standard artillery weapons for the Royal Marines.*

a British design of gun which has incorporated the best features of the famous 25-pounder filed Howitzer and the German 88 mm anti-tank of the Second World War.

The gun weighs about 2 tonnes and fires a 35 lb (15.9 kg) round some 17 km (10.6 statute miles), being manned by a crew of six. It can fire high explosive (HE), airburst HE, armour piercing anti-tank, screening smoke, illumination and target indicating rounds. The rate of fire is 30 shells a minute.

There is a large muzzle brake which reduces recoil shock and it has been designed to give the gun crew ease of access to the breech, using a bowed towing trail which is hitched to a 1 tonne Land Rover (powered by the Range Rover V8 petrol engine) or similar tug. For normal towing the barrel folds over the trail. The gun can be fitted with skis and towed behind the Volvo BV 202E tracked vehicle, giving the weapon a limited cross-country mobility over snow-covered terrain. The 105 mm Light Gun and the 1 tonne Land Rover can both be transported by air beneath the Sea King HC 4, Puma HC 1 or the gun only, in two pieces under the Wessex HU 5.

Six guns are deployed to each Commando Battery, making a total of 18 guns in 29 Commando Light Regiment Royal Artillery.

HELICOPTERS

Although there were a number of Royal Marines pilots during the Second World War, and subsequently as aircrew with the Royal Navy's Fleet Air Arm, it was not until 1968 that the Royal Marines formed its own Brigade Squadron. Helicopters have been a part of Royal Marines flying ever since.

Four types have been used by the 3 Commando Brigade Air Squadron (see page 69) since the late 1960s, initially the Bell (West-land) Sioux and later the Westland Scout, some armed with Nord SS11 wire-guided missiles for anti-tank duties. Following the re-equipment programme for the Army Air Corps, 3 Cdo Bde Air Sqn has received the Gazelle (from 1978) and the Lynx/TOW (from 1983) for its support role.

AEROSPATIALE GAZELLE AH 1

Purpose *Light observation, reconnaissance and liaison;* **Crew** *1 pilot, 1 aircrewman;* **Passengers** *Up to 4;* **Maiden flight** *2 August 1968 (prototype), 31 January 1972 (SA 341B);* **Service entry** *1973 (AAC); 1978 (RM);* **Range** *362 nm (670 km);* **Max speed** *143 kt (264 km/h);* **Cruising speed** *120 kt (222 km/h);* **Service ceiling** *16,400 ft (5,000 m);* **Hover in Ground Effect** *9,350 ft (2,850 m);* **Rate of climb** *1,770 ft/min (9 m/s);* **Length** *31,27 ft (9.53 m);* **Height** *8.94 ft (2.72 m);* **Rotor diameter** *34.46 ft (10.5 m);* **Power plant** *1 x Turbomeca Astazou IIIN2 (643 hp);* **Weapons** *None standard but has provision for pod-mountings of machine guns, 68 mm rockets, Spectrolab Nightsun lamp and other aids;* **All-up weight** *4,189 lb (1,900 kg);* **Empty weight** *1,874 lb (850 kg);* **Payload** *2,026 lb (918 kg).*

Aerospatiale Gazelle AH 1 from 3 Cdo Bde Sqn RM. The aircrew is trained by the Army Air Corps, with whom the airframes are pooled. RM helicopters generally operate with the flotation bags fitted (the 'canvas' bags on the skids). Recent equipment updates include the Ferranti Gazelle Observation Aid.

The British procurement of the SA341B Gazelle resulted from the 1967 Anglo-French Helicopter agreement, which also produced the Lynx and Puma. By this arrangement, the Aerospatiale design was partially manufactured and completely assembled by Westland Helicopters at Yeovil and Weston-super-Mare. The initial production contract was for 29 helicopters, delivered between April 1973 and September 1974, and eventually some 212 were delivered. The first unit to be equipped was 660 Squadron AAC and the last airframe was delivered in 1984.

The Gazelle is a front-line observation helicopter, now equipped with the Ferranti AF 532 observation aid (known as GOA to the 3 Cdo Bde Air Sqn and Army Air Corps) which operates with the Lynx/TOW in HELARM (Helicopter Armed Action) teams, designed to blunt the advance of enemy armour, especially in the Northern Flank operational area of Norway.

In addition, Gazelle helicopters have been attached to Royal Marines detachments around the world, including Cyprus, the Far East and Belize, and to Commando Groups serving a tour in Northern Ireland. The helicopters are used for liaison, forward reconnaissance border patrol, personnel transportation, casualty evacuation and specialist reconnaissance tasks. In Northern Ireland, the Gazelle has a variety of special tasks, including aerial cover for street patrols, carrying the Spectrolab Nightsun searchlight and acting as a fast communications aircraft for military and government personnel.

During the Falklands conflict, some Gazelles of 3 Cdo Bde Air

Westland Lynx AH 1, armed with the Hughes Aircraft TOW anti-tank missile. The helicopter can also be used to transport troops and Milan missile teams to set up blocking actions against enemy armoured thrusts.

Sqn were armed with SNEB 68 mm rocket pods (similar to the ground attack Harrier) to give some measure of self-protection, but in the event, the weapons were not used. In addition, cabin-mounted 7.62 mm General Purpose Machine Guns were carried. The SNEB is not, however, considered a standard weapon. Nevertheless, the helicopter proved its worth during Operation Corporate, although two were lost to Argentine ground fire during the first day of the San Carlos landings.

Both Gazelle AH 1 and Lynx AH 1 airframes from Army Air Corps stocks are assigned to the 3rd Commando Brigade Air Squadron at RNAS Yeovilton, Somerset.

WESTLAND LYNX AH 1

Purpose *Anti-tank, liaison and command;* **Crew** *1 pilot/aircrewman, 1 pilot/aircraft commander;* **Passengers** *Up to 9;* **Maiden flight** *12 April 1972 (prototype), 11 February 1977 (production);* **Service entry** *1977 (AAC), 1983 (RM);* **Range** *340 nm (630 km);* **Max speed** *140 kt (259 km/h);* **Cruising speed** *125 kt (232 km/h);* **Service ceiling** *12,000 ft (3,660 m);* **Hover in Ground Effect** *NA;* **Rate of climb** *2,170 ft/min (11 m/s);* **Length** *43.63 ft (13.3 m);* **Height** *11.5 ft (3.5 m);* **Rotor diameter** *42 ft (12.8 m);* **Weapons** *8 x TOW anti-tank missiles; podded machine gun option (see text);* **Powerplant** *2 x Rolls-Royce Gem 2 turboshafts (900 shp each);* **All-up weight** *9,600 lb (4,355 kg);* **Empty weight** *6,773 lb (3,072 kg);* **Payload** *3,894 lb (1,766 kg).*

The initial concept of the Westland WG 13 Lynx was as a utility helicopter to carry squad-sized infantry, armed with anti-tank, mortar and other direct fire weapons. In this role, the helicopter was due to replace the Scout. With the adoption of the concept of the Scout/SS 11 missile combination, the role envisaged for the Lynx changed to that of primarily anti-tank helicopter, working in concert with the Gazelle (see above) as a highly effective and flexible blocking strike force.

For the Royal Marines, the Lynx/TOW represents the only readily tactical-directed and rapid response anti-armour weapon. The main area of operation in wartime would be Norway, and 3 Cdo Bde Air Sqn regularly trains in that country, as well as taking its helicopters on exercises to other countries to test and develop tactics for any eventuality. Lynx, equipped with special wheels are capable of operation from aircraft carriers, assault ships and other warships, or from the decks of ships taken up from trade. The TOW weapon is interchangeable with Army Air Corps and some NATO allies' equipment.

The Lynx is crewed by the aircraft captain, who under the new manning arrangements agreed with the Army Air Corps is seated in the left-hand seat, controlling the TOW Roof Sight, which is soon to be upgraded with a Rank Pullin Controls thermal imaging module for night and adverse weather operations. The aircraft captain is in command of the helicopter and directs the pilot, usually a non-commissioned officer, who is in the right-hand seat of the helicopter.

There is accommodation in the helicopter's rear cabin for up to eight fully-equipped personnel. The helicopter could be used to land commandos behind enemy lines or to carry a ground-mounted anti-tank team with Milan or similar weapons. The Lynx can be used for casualty evacuation and has limited search and rescue facilities.

RAIDING AND SMALL CRAFT

Besides the landing craft more traditionally associated with the Royal Marines and described above, there are a number of highly specialized small craft which are in everyday use.

FERRYMAN 18

Length 5.48 *m*; **Beam** 2.21 *m*; **Draught** 0.40 *m*; **Displacement** 2.5 *tonnes*; **Crew** *Coxswain + 2*; **Capacity** *10 troops*; **Engine** *1 x OMC petrol outboard (140 bhp)*; **Speed** *20 knots.*

Three were ordered in May 1984 from Freezer Aluminium Boats of Hayling Island and entered service in August 1984. Designed as a

A dusk landing by a special assault party from 42 Commando using a rigid raider (Greg Ferguson).

new type of raiding craft for the Royal Marines, they are of aluminium construction using rigid inflatable techniques.

DELL QUAY RIGID RAIDER

Length 5.2 m; **Beam** 2.2 m; **Height** 1.1 m; **Draught** 0.25 m; **Weight** 590 kg; **Crew** Coxswain; **Capacity** 6 to 9 troops; **Engine** 1 or 2 x Johnson outboard(s) (140 bhp each); **Speed** 35 knots plus.

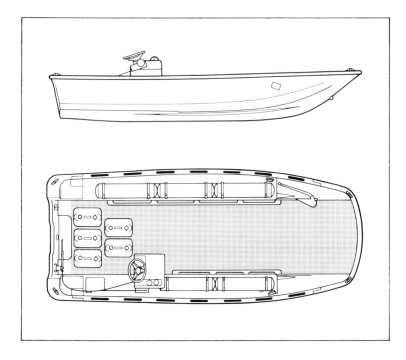

Constructed of glass-reinforced plastic, unsinkable and able to penetrate high surf, the Rigid Raider is modelled on the Dory 17 hull. The normal complement is the coxswain, often dressed in special protective gear, trained and operating as part of a Raiding Squadron, and up to nine Royal Marine Commandos. Inflatable passenger bags can be fitted. For storage, Rigid Raider hulls can be stacked three high.

PACIFIC 22/SEARIDER SR 3M

Length *5.43 m*; **Beam** *2.03 m*; **Weight** *300 kg, 495 kg (operating)*; **Displacement** *2,450 tonnes (dry), 1.545 tonnes (swamped)*; **Crew** *Coxswain and radio operator*; **Capacity** *10 troops or 750 kg cargo*; **Engine** *1 or 2 x Johnson outboard(s) (90 hp each)*; **Speed** *40 knots.*

Designed as a rigid-hull inflatable craft to give resilience and yet be portable enough for Royal Marines and Royal Naval operations. Replaced the Rigid Raider with 3 Raiding Squadron, Royal Marines in Hong Kong during the initial anti-illegal immigrant operations which were developed into anti-smuggler operations in 1980-88.

Operationally in Hong Kong waters, many successful chases and arrests have been made using the craft. The normal pattern is to operate four or five together, co-ordinated by a Royal Hong Kong Police launch or RN patrol craft, keeping in contact by radio and on radar as the craft have special radar reflectors fitted.

3 Raiding Squadron Royal Marines, which disbanded in 1988, used the Avon 3m Searider for anti-illegal immigrant, 'boat people' and smuggler patrols from Hong Kong.

AVON GEMINI

Length *4.62 m;* **Beam** *1.9 m;* **Weight** *144 kg;* **Displacement** *2.5 tonnes (dry),*
1.8 tonnes (swamped); **Max payload** *954 kg or 10 troops;* **Engine** *1 x 40 hp out-*
board; **Speed** *18 knots;* **Dimensions for transport** *176 x 89 x 54 mm.*

DUNLOP GEMINI

Length *4.6 m;* **Weight** *137.4 kg; other data as for the Avon Gemini.*

This famous assault, patrol and supply light craft is manufactured to
Ministry of Defence specification by two major sub-contractors better known in the United Kingdom as manufacturers of road tyres.
The 10-man assault version is used by the Royal Marines and 6-man
patrol type is in service with the Royal Navy, replacing ships' boats
on many major warships.

Gemini raiding craft are operated by 2 Raiding Squadron, Royal
Marines Reserve. Easily transported by road, air and sea, the Gemini
can be re-inflated and re-built within 30 minutes.

KLEPPER CANOE

Length *5.36 m;* **Beam** *0.91 m;* **Weight** *50.8 kg (dry).*

The famous two-man canoe of the Royal Marines Special Boat
Squadron was adapted from a German design and has been in use
for many years without any replacement. It is used for reconnaissance and clandestine raiding, being launched from helicopters,
landing craft or partially submerged submarines.

During the Borneo confrontation with Indonesia, Klepper
canoes were used for riverway patrols, being sturdy enough to cope
with rapids and other obstacles.

LANDING CRAFT

Landing craft have been an important part of the Royal Marines,
amphibious capability since the Second World War. Two basic types
of landing craft are now in service: Landing Craft Utility (LCU) and
Landing Craft Vehicle and Personnel (LCVP). In addition there is a

The LSL (Landing Ship Logistic) RFA Sir Bedivere at anchor with equipment stored on its forward helicopter deck and one of HMS Fearless' LCU Mk 9s using the aft cargo door to transfer stores.

class of Landing Craft Personnel (Light) (LCP(L)). Other Royal Marines water craft are described separately.

Landing Craft Utility were formerly known as Landing Craft Mechanized and although a primary function is still to land vehicles from the LPDs *Fearless* and *Intrepid*, the craft are also capable of independent operations, especially in northern Norway and the Northern European Command (NEC) area.

LCUs have a limited beach assault role in the conventional sense although the craft figured in the landings on San Carlos Water during the Falklands conflict. They can be used to land vehicles as large as Main Battle Tanks and lorries, but also for carrying large numbers of Royal Marines (under cover if conditions dictate), logistical resupply and casualty evacuation. Since 1980-81, winter season trials have been carried out by LCUs acting independently in Norway, including unescorted North Sea Crossings from Scotland.

LCU MK 9

Length 25.7 m; **Beam** 6.5 m; **Draught** 1.7 m; **Displacement** 76,272 tonnes (unladen), 178, 985 tonnes (full load); **Crew** Colour Sergeant + 6; **Capacity** 100 tonnes of cargo, vehicles or personnel; **Engines** 2 x Paxman YHXAM diesels (312 bhp each), nozzle propellers; **Speed** 10 knots (19 km/h); **Sensors** Decca 101 I-band navigation radar.

L700–L702 built by Brooke Marine, Lowestoft; L703 lost in the Falklands, 8 June 1982; L704–L709 built by Richard Dunston,

One of the Vosper Thornycroft-built Landing Crafts Utility Mk 9, used by the Amphibious Trials and Training Unit at Instow (hence the AT code).

Thorne; L710–L711 built by J. Bolson, Poole; L3507–L3508 built by Vosper.

Fearless and *Intrepid* are complemented for four LCUs each, carrying the identification letters F for *Fearless* and T for *Intrepid*. Four training craft are based at RM Poole and carry the identification letter P.

LCVP MKS 1, 2 and 3

Length *12.7 m;* **Beam** *3.1 m;* **Draught** *0.8 m;* **Displacement** *8,644 tonnes, 13.73 tonnes (full load);* **Crew** *Corporal + 2;* **Capacity** *35 troops or 2 x ½ tonne Land Rovers (1 x ½ tonne Land Rover if launched from ship's davits);* **Engines** *2 x Foden diesels (126 bhp each);* **Speed** *10 knots, 8 knots (loaded).*
Hull numbers:
Mk 1 102, 112, 118, 120, 123, 127, 128, 134, 136
Mk 2 142 – 149
Mk 3 150 – 158

Fearless and *Intrepid* carry four each of the LCVP Mk 2 design from davits amidships. The remaining Mk 1 craft are used for training and general utility roles; the Royal Corps of Transport operates a number of former RM Landing Craft for logistical re-supply operations, including a number Mk 1 and Mk 3 craft. For operations in northern Norway these craft are camouflaged and it is understood that they will be gradually replaced by the Mk 4 craft during the next five years.

During Operation Corporate, four LCVPs were converted for

mines countermeasures work in San Carlos and later Port
Stanley.

LCVP MK 4

Length *13.0 m;* **Beam** *3.2 m;* **Draught** *0.80 m;* **Displacement** *10 tonnes;* **Crew**
Corporal + *2;* **Capacity** *35 troops or 5.5 tonnes of cargo;* **Engines** *2 x Perkins 76–*
3544 diesels (220 hp each); **Speed** *20 knots, 16 knots (loaded);* **Range** *200 nm at*
12 knots; **Sensors** *I-band navigation radar.*

One was built by Fairey Allday Marine, Hample and delivered in
1982, fourteen more have been delivered by W. A. Souter of
Cowes, from February 1985 to September 1986. The design uses
aluminium construction and is an Admiralty design resulting from
extensive tests carried out at ATTRUM Instow to replace the LCVP
Mks 1, 2 and 3 types which have been in service for some
years.

LCP (L)

Length *11.3 m;* **Beam** *3.4 m;* **Draught** *1.0 m;* **Displacement** *6.5 tonnes, 10 ton-*
nes (full load); **Crew** *Coxswain* + *2;* **Capacity** *35 troops or 3.5 tonnes cargo;*
Engines *2 x Paxman diesels (225 bhp each);* **Speed** *12 knots, 8 knots*
(loaded).

Four of the Souter-built Landing Crafts Vehicle and Personnel Mk 4s which have been
successfully deployed in Norway, especially with 539 Assault Squadron Royal Marines
(RM/CPO Holdgate).

A beach-head established during a training exercise near Lee-on-Solent shows a mexi-flote acting as a floating dock for stores and equipment, with an LCU Mk 9 alongside. The beach-head is organized by Commando Logistic Regiment (Patrick Allen).

Hull nos. 501, 503 and 556 are operated with Royal Navy crews for utility tasks, and could be made available to the Royal Marines in the event of war.

LCM MK 7

Length *18.4 m;* **Beam** *4.9 m;* **Draught** *1.2 m;* **Displacement** *Not available;* **Crew** *Coxswain + 5;* **Capacity** *100 tonnes;* **Engines** *2 x Gray diesels (290 bhp each);* **Speed** *10 knots;* **Sensors** *Navigation radar.*

7037 and 7100 are former British Army landing craft of the Landing Craft Mechanized Mk 7 type which are still used by the Royal Navy for auxiliary and training roles. In the event of war, they could be made available to the Royal Marines.

MEXIFLOTE

Self-propelled low-freeboard pontoons used to transport troops, vehicles and equipment ashore. They are powered by two Sykes Marine Harbourmaster F725 engines of 150 hp each, but these will be replaced by Ford 2725 diesels in due course, following an order in 1985.

These craft are lashed to the side of the 'Sir Bedevere' Class LSLs and were used extensively in the Falklands conflict. 35 or more are in service with the Royal Marines, with additional craft available to the British Army.

ROYAL MARINES VEHICLES

As has been explained previously, it is not possible to list all the RM vehicles, but the following have been selected as the most commonly operated by uniformed RM personnel. The reference used is the NATO vehicle code and the titles are those used by the Royal Marines, rather than the British Army or the Royal Navy.

There are no fighting vehicles in the RM and only one armoured vehicle, because unlike the USMC, for example, the RM are highly mobile on foot, by skis or by helicopter. The Northern Flank does not lend itself to armoured operations in any case. Command Vehicles are usually Land Rovers and/or tents. In Cyprus, whilst on United Nations duties, the RM does have the use of British Army-supplied, UN-marked Ferret scout cars for secure transportation, but these are outside the scope of this book. The one exception to the armoured vehicle non-operation policy is the BARV:

The vehicle deck of HMS Fearless *during amphibious operations shows some of the vehicles available to the Corps for landing operations. In the centre, beneath the vehicle ramp, is a BARV, a Michigan with Class M trackway alongside (left) and a range of Land Rovers and their trailers to the right. In the foreground are two of the LPD's four LCU Mk 9s.*

To assist beaching operations, the Royal Marines use the Beach Armoured Recovery Vehicle, based on the chassis of a main battle tank, for pulling vehicles and even landing craft ashore.

VA0540* BEACH ARMOURED RECOVERY VEHICLE (BARV)

Armament *1 x 7.62 mm L4A4 Machine Gun;* **Crew** *4;* **Weight in action** *40,643 kg;* **Length** *8.076 m;* **Height** *3.453 m;* **Width** *3.402 m;* **Track width** *0.61 m;* **Ground clearance** *0.5 m;* **Maximum road speed** *34.6 km/h;* **Range (roads)** *64.5 km;* **Engine type** *Rolls-Royce Meteor Mark IVB;* **Engine Power** *650 bhp;* **Engine capacity** *27 litres;* **Fuel capacity** *550 litres;* **Ammunition capacity** *7.62 mm–400 rounds.*

The BARV is based on a Centurion MBT and was designed in the early 1960s to assist stranded vehicles during amphibious operations, being able to wade to a depth of 2.9 m. Most of the LPD/LSL vessels which provide amphibious lift for the RM have at least one BARV on their complement, but with the diminution of the Marine assault role and the experience that the BARV is not all it was designed to be, many of the vehicles have passed into Army hands for service with the British Army of the Rhine.

*NATO parlance denotes VA as Vehicle Armoured and VB as Vehicle Second Line.

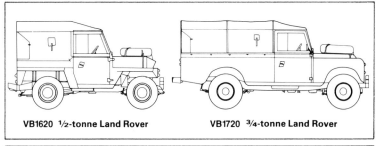

VB1620 ½-tonne Land Rover   VB1720 ¾-tonne Land Rover

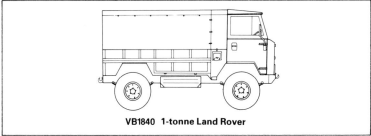

VB1840 1-tonne Land Rover

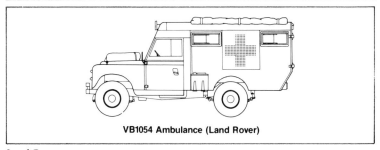

VB1054 Ambulance (Land Rover)

Land Rover variations.   1:76 scale

VB1620 ½-TONNE LAND ROVER TRUCK UTILITY 4 x 4

Crew *1 + 2*; **Weight loaded** *2,018 kg*; **Length** *3.632 m*; **Height** *1.95 m*; **Width** *1.524 m*; **Wheel track** *1.308 m*; **Ground clearance** *0.21 m*; **Maximum road speed** *105 km/h*; **Range on roads** *560–600 km*; **Engine type** *Rover 4-cylinder OHV*; **Engine power** *77 bhp*; **Engine capacity** *2.286 litres*; **Fuel capacity** *91 litres.*

The ubiquitous Land Rover is used at all levels of the RM, including Headquarters, Mortar Troops and Signals Troops. The usual complement of this vehicle in a Commando is 48 with a similar number of ¾-tonne trailers. It is air-portable by the Wessex HU 5 (when stripped to lighten the load), or with trailer by the new Sea King HC 4.

Deliveries began in 1968 and the vehicle is well liked for its good four-wheel drive performance and comfort. There are two variants, dependent on radio fit—12v and 24v. Other features include convoy lights and the ability to operate the 'Rover without any lights burning.

The normal paint scheme is drab dark green and black, but there are a number of RM vehicles in standard Navy blue with white 'ROYAL MARINES' legends on the side doors. Petrol-driven engines are commonly used for, despite fire risk when carried at sea, especially on the deck of an LPD or CVS, they can be bump-started in the field. The reinforced bumpers assist with starting and pushing.

VB1720 ¾-TONNE LAND ROVER TRUCK UTILITY FFR 4 x 4

Crew *1 + 2-8;* **Weight loaded** *2,620 kg;* **Length** *4.648 m;* **Height** *2.057 m;* **Width** *1,689 m;* **Wheel track** *1.308 m;* **Ground clearance** *0.228 m;* **Maximum road speed** *88 km/h;* **Range (roads)** *450/500 km;* **Engine type** *Rover 4-cylinder OHV;* **Engine power** *77 bhp;* **Engine capacity** *2.286 litres;* **Fuel capacity** *91 litres.*

The long wheelbase Land Rover has been in production for many years and is a general carrier for the RM, but in much smaller scale use than the half-tonner because they are not so readily air portable. Generally, the ¾-tonne is used at RM barracks and for exercises. There are a number serving with the RMR as supply vehicles. They can be fitted with hard or soft tops, with or without radios, as plain troop transports or for more specialist work. They are not, however, as good as the ½-tonne version in cross-country work, being heavier for the same power.

VB1054 AMBULANCE 4-STRETCHER MEDIUM MOBILITY 4 x 4

Crew *1–2;* **Weight in action** *2,670 kg;* **Length** *4.826 m;* **Height** *2.146 m;* **Width** *1.905 m;* **Wheel track** *1.308 m;* **Maximum road speed** *96 km/h;* **Range (roads)** *450 km;* **Engine type** *Rover 2.5;* **Engine power** *77 bhp;* **Engine capacity** *2.286 litres;* **Fuel capacity** *90.86 litres.*

This is the ambulance version of the ¾-tonne Land Rover which has been developed by Marshall of Cambridge for use by the Army and RM. It has seen service in Northern Ireland and elsewhere, including the Northern Flank areas. Basically, the long wheelbase Land Rover has been fitted with a new aluminium body to take four Service stretchers and a sitting attendant. The stretchers can be folded away for the accommodation of sitting casualties. The vehicle is finished in olive drab or olive drab and black, with prominent red crosses.

VB1840 1-TONNE LAND ROVER TRUCK SI SERVICE 4 x 4

Crews *1 + 1–8;* **Weight loaded** *3,120 kg;* **Length** *4.127 m;* **Height** *2.138 m;* **Width** *1.842 m;* **Wheel track (front)** *1.524 m;* **Wheel track (rear)** *1.549 m;* **Ground clearance** *0.254 m;* **Maximum road speed** *120 km/h;* **Range (roads)** *560 km;* **Engine type** *Rover V8;* **Engine power** *128 bhp;* **Engine capacity** *3.5 litres;* **Fuel capacity** *109 litres.*

The 1-tonne Land Rover was jointly developed by British Leyland's Rover subsidiary and the Motor Vehicle Experimental Establishment for an Army and RM requirement. The vehicle is air-portable by Sea King HC 4 and is used in considerable numbers. It is found in service with Anti-Tank Troops and as a tug for the 105 mm Light Guns of 29 Commando Light Regiment. It can operate with 81 mm mortar team and is fitted with a 12v electrical system.

A standard vehicle is the 1-tonne Land Rover (Forward Control), seen here with its trailer. It can be carried beneath a support helicopter for amphibious landings (RM/PO Phot Campbell).

VB2025 BEDFORD MK 4-TONNE TRUCK CARGO 4 x 4

Crew 1 + 2; **Weight loaded** 9,650 *kg*; **Length** 6.579 *m*; **Height (top of cab)** 2.501 *m*; **Height (tarpaulin)** 3.404 *m*; **Width** 2.489 *m*; **Wheel track (front)** 2.05 *m*; **Wheel track (rear)** 2.03 *m*; **Maximum road speed** 73 *km/h*; **Range (roads)** 560 *km*; **Engine type** *Bedford 6-cylinder*; **Engine power** 106 *bhp*; **Engine capacity** 5.42 *litres*; **Fuel capacity** 150 *litres*; **Load area** 4.28 x 2.01 *m*.

The highly successful Bedford MK 4-tonne truck has all but completely replaced the Bedford RL Truck which had been produced in large numbers for all the British Armed Forces. It is seen in two main variants: the Bedford EJN which is a commercial transport for driver training at RM Poole and for limited road-work; and the cross-country 4 x 4 MK with its characteristic drab paint finish. Actually, several MK models are painted Navy Blue with the 'ROYAL MARINES' legend for recruiting (with Recruit Company, RM Poole).

The basic role of the 4-tonner in RM service is as a Rifle Company transport and support vehicle with the B echelon (stores). A typical Commando will have between 15 and 20 MKs on strength. Other typical uses of the cargo, soft or hard top truck are to transport the Assault Engineer Troop and to provide mobility and transport to the Commando HQ.

There are three basic variants of the MK in service with the RM: VB2050 4-tonne truck with winch; VB2091 4-tonne truck with flat platform; and VB2204 4-tonne truck with bulk fuel. The flat bed truck can have a number of special containers fitted which include provision of a workshop for the RM's craftsmen. The bulk fuel adaption is widely used to support RN and RM helicopters in the field and during training sorties/exercises on such places as Salisbury Plain. These vehicles are often manned by RN personnel.

BEDFORD MK CRANE AND FLAT

Crew 1+ 2; **Weight** 9,000 *kg (approx)*; **Length** 6.36 *m*; **Height (top of cab)** 2.602 *m*; **Width** 2.39 *m*; **Wheel track** 1.854 *m*; **Maximum road speed** 72.4 *km/h*; **Range (roads)** 402.3 *km*; **Engine type** *Bedford 6-cylinder*; **Engine power** 130 *bhp*; **Engine capacity** 4.93 *litres*; **Load area** 4.27 x 2.18 *m*.

The Bedford Crane and Flat Bed truck is based on the standard 4 x 4 Bedford 4-tonne chassis and can be used to transport small craft, including Raiding Craft and Motor Dories, or Gemini.

BEDFORD RL (4 x 4) 4-TONNE TRUCK

Crew *1 + 1*; **Weight loaded** *8,800 kg*; **Length** *6.36 m*; **Height (top of cab)** *2.602 m*; **Height (tarpaulin)** *3.11 m*; **Width** *2.39 m*; **Wheel track** *1.854 m*; **Maximum road speed** *75 km/h*; **Range (roads)** *400 km*; **Engine type** *Bedford 6-cylinder OHV*; **Engine power** *130 bhp*; **Engine capacity** *4.93 litres*; **Fuel capacity** *118 litres*; **Load area** *4.267 x 2.178 m*.

Although now largely superseded by the MK, the venerable Bedford RL continues to soldier on in a variety of guises.

WATER TANKERS

The RM, like all Services, needs water for everyday needs. Marines are particularly fussy about washing and cooking, maintaining that one can only fight well when completely fit, and this includes well fed and clean: 'why else are the Army's troops called Pongos?. . . '

The Corps has 1- and 3-tonne water carriers, both trailer-borne and self-propelled. One will be found with each Commando, probably at the Commando HQ.

MOTOR CYCLES

The RM still operates motor cycles as war machines and for convoy escort work. The current bikes are the Canam Bombardier for combat and the Triumph Tiger with Polaris fairing for convoy work and driver training. The latter is carried out at RM Poole. Kawasaki 'scramblers' were also used during the drive on Port Stanley in May/ June 1982.

UTILITY VEHICLES

As in any organization which needs to be mobile and to carry personnel and light equipment around the countryside, the RM has a number of utility ('tilly') type vehicles which are usually found at

RM centres and barracks. The Bedford Sherpa is extensively used, usually in an RM blue scheme with the Corps legend on the side. The RM also use Naval vehicles which are designated Car Utility Large 1144–4828. In addition, there are a large number of commercial cars used, the Ford Granada and Cortina as staff cars and the Ford Escort Estate BL Mini for personnel transportation.

RECOVERY VEHICLES

There are a number of light and medium recovery vehicles operated by the RM in uniform, including the former Army FV13115 Recovery Vehicle Wheeled which uses a Bedford RL chassis. Many of these vehicles, although available to the Royal Marines, are operated by Army units and thus are outside the scope of this book.

SPECIALIST VEHICLES

VC7765 TRACTOR, WHEELED, FORK LIFT 4,000 lb—ROUGH TERRAIN

Crew 1; **Weight complete** 2,961 *kg;* **Weight air-portable** 2,560 *kg;* **Length** 5.461 *m;* **Height (fork raised to maximum)** 3.708 *m;* **Height (top of mast)** 2.388; **Height (air-portable)** 1.829 *m;* **Width** 1.854 *m;* **Wheel track** 1.55 *m;* **Maximum road speed** 64 *km/h;* **Range (roads)** 644 *km;* **Range (cross-country)** 322 *km;* **Engine type** *Perkins 4-236 diesel;* **Engine power** 78 *bhp;* **Engine capacity** 3.8 *litres;* **Fuel capacity** *Unknown;* **Maximum lift** 1,814 *kg.*

Moving across its own class M trackway to enable vehicles to move up a shingle beach is the Michigan tractor operated by a Royal Corps of Transport element within Commando Logistic Regiment.

The Eager Beaver cross-country fork-lift with a load of petrol jerry-cans and driven by a member of the Commando Logistic Regiment.

One of the strangest specialist vehicles, used for amphibious operations and for general purpose duties at RM barracks, is the Eager Beaver wheeled fork lift. The vehicle can ford 0.76 m so can be used to transfer materials from a landing craft to the beach, or on river crossings. The fork lift part is adjustable and is laid back 60° for air transport in a C-130K Hercules C 1 or C 3 RAF transport aircraft, or underslung from a Sea King HC 4. In the Northern Flank operating areas, the Eager Beaver is fitted with a cab for driver protection. The Royal Corps of Transport also use this vehicle for a similar purpose of laying Class 30 trackway.

VB1260 CARRIER FULL TRACKED ARCTIC LHD

Armament 1 x 7.62 mm L7A2 Machine-Gun (if fitted); **Crew** 2 + 8-10; **Weight in action** 4,200 kg; **Length** 6.172 m; **Height** 2.21 m; **Width** 1.759 m; **Ground clearance** 0.3 m; **Maximum road speed** 39 km/h; **Range (roads)** 400 km; **Engine type** Volvo type B18 petrol; **Engine power** 91 bhp; **Engine capacity** 1.78 litres; **Fuel capacity** 156 litres.

The Volvo Bv202 is a Swedish-designed over-snow vehicle which has been adopted by the RM and the British Army since 1968. The vehicle can be used to draw the 105 mm Light Gun, an Articulated Passage Compartment or stores carriers, and is frequently seen with a section of ski-troops in tow. Because its use is restricted to Norway, except for a few training models, the Bv202 is left-hand drive (LHD) and is used for cross-country work. If the Articulated

The replacement for the ubiquitous and trusted BV 202 is the improved oversnow vehicle, designated BV 206, seen here during trials in Norway. The picture shows the tractor half of the combination only (RM).

Passage Compartment has a soft top, this can be opened to give a cargo area of 2.3 x 1.56 m. The Bv202 is air-portable under a Sea King HC 4. The general appearance of these vehicles is white with occasionally dark green/black camouflage patterns painted overall. The vehicle was used on East Falkland, especially around Goose Green and San Carlos. A new version is to be ordered.

Bv206

As part of a vehicle re-equipment plan, the Royal Marines have acquired and will acquire more Volvo Bv206 arctic carriers. Currently, the vehicles have been assigned to the Commando Helicopter Operations Cell for trials but future deliveries will continue until 1990. Full details have yet to be made available.

VEHICLE SUMMARY

A typical Rifle Company of the Royal Marines will probably have the following vehicles on strength: 2 x ½-tonne Land Rovers and 1 x 4-tonne Bedford truck. A Mortar Troop, on the other hand, has a considerable amount of kit to move around and the following could be typical: 2 x ½-tonne Land Rovers and 7 x 1-tonne Land Rovers. A Commando Brigade could be considered fully equipped with 500 vehicles and 400 trailers.

UNIFORMS, BADGES AND RANK STRUCTURE

Perhaps because it is a special type of force, the Corps of the Royal Marines has an unusual situation in respect of its uniforms, badges and ranks. Outwardly, the Corps dresses like the British Army and receives much of its equipment from that service; at the same time it is part of the Royal Navy, yet has its own traditions, badges, ceremonial and folklore.

ROYAL MARINES UNIFORM

All ranks up to and including lieutenant-colonel wear the insignia 'RM' in gilt on their shoulder straps and all ranks wear the globe and laurel collar badges which are directly comparable to whatever cap badge is worn.

Above *Gilt shoulder insignia.*
Above right *Collar badge.*

Right *A former commanding officer of 40 Commando, Lieutenant Colonel (now Colonel) Timothy Donkin MBE RM, is pictured wearing the Royal Marines' coveted green beret, the shoulder insignia (crown and star) of a Lieutenant Colonel and the RM insignia. His right shoulder lanyard is light blue denoting 40 Cdo, the left shoulder lanyard is the officer's dark blue.*

Cap Badge This was presented to the Corps in 1923 when the Royal Marines Light Infantry and Royal Marine Artillery amalgamated. Officers and warrant officers wear a two-part badge with the lion/crown emblem separate from the globe surrounded by the laurel; only the Warrant Officer 2 has a gilt globe, the others are silver. Bronze or cloth badges are worn with combat dress.

Blue uniform This is the famous ceremonial uniform of the Royal Marines. Officers wear a blue tunic and trouser combination of a similar pattern to officers' khaki service dress in the British Army. Officers have plain-bottomed trousers with a thin scarlet stripe (called a welt) down each outside seam of the trousers up to the rank of colonel. Full colonel and above have a broader stripe. The trousers are tight-fitting, similar to overalls in appearance, worn over leather wellington boots. From the rank of major (field officer) and above, spurs are worn.

Traditional headgear for ceremonial occasions is the remarkable Wolseley-pattern white helmet with brass ball top, helmet plate and chin stay. It has been worn by officers and other ranks since the early part of the twentieth century.

Other ranks also wear blue to a pattern confirmed in 1923 but which has been improved since the mid 1970s. For other ranks, the cut and material of the suit has been replaced with a blue tweed, and the trousers have a narrow scarlet stripe down the outside seam of each leg.

Mess Dress This is peculiar to the Royal Marines, worn by officers, warrant officers and senior non-commissioned officers wearing No 1s during regular mess dining nights and other functions.

The present Commandant General of the Royal Marines, Lieutenant General Sir Martin Garrod KCB OBE, when commanding 3 Commando Brigade RM in the rank of Brigadier. He is wearing the distinctive Lovat uniform, green beret (with lion and crown) and shoulder rank insignia (crown and three stars). His jacket bears the red British Army gorget lapel patches which denote senior officer status of Colonel and above.

Right *Warrant Officers 2 and above wear the 'split' cap badge with the lion and crown separate from the globe and laurel.*

Warrant Officer 2

Lovat uniform The attractive green and khaki interweave of the Lovat uniform is unique to the Corps and was first worn in April 1964, replacing the wartime-type battle dress or second suit of blues. Lovat mackintoshes are worn by all ranks.

Great coats Until 1986, Royal Marines wore a khaki great coat with a distinctive arrangement of buttons in four pairs. This has now been replaced by a similar pattern Navy blue great coat.

Green beret This coveted and important insignia of the Royal Marines denotes a Commando-trained officer or man. The beret was introduced in 1942 and has been worn by Commandos ever since. Bandsmen (except the Band of the Royal Marine Commandos) and recruits wear a blue beret.

Lanyards When in lovat dress, unit lanyards are worn by all Commando ranks, on the right shoulder:

HQ Cdo Forces:	blue
Cdo Log Regt:	blue
HQ 3 Cdo Bde:	dark green
40 Cdo:	light blue
42 Cdo:	white
45 Cdo:	scarlet
Comacchio Company:	gold/scarlet

Officers and Warrant Officer 1s wear a navy blue silk lanyard on their left shoulder. This is one way of distinguishing a general officer of the Royal Marines.

Gorget patches These are British Army pattern scarlet and denote a senior officer of colonel and above. They are worn at the collar of shirts, lapels of jackets and even DPM (Disruptive Pattern Material) combat dress.

General Officers

Brigadiers and Colonels

BADGES OF RANK

Although only a small Corps by the standards of other armed services, the Royal Marines has a full rank structure to lieutenant general or NATO 3-Star level. In addition, there are other senior appointments, some of which are mainly ceremonial but nevertheless play an important role in today's Royal Marines.

Captain General This is a post which dates back to the sixteenth century and which in the past has held considerable power. In 1953, HRH The Prince Philip succeeded his late Majesty King George VI as the Captain General, appointed so by the Queen. Prince Philip holds the rank of Field Marshal, outside the normal structure of the Royal Marines. As Captain General, he is regularly informed about the Corps and there was considerable press speculation about his concern when HRH Prince Edward resigned from the Corps in January 1987.

The Captain General of the Royal Marines is HRH The Prince Philip, Duke of Edinburgh, who was appointed in succession to the last King George VI in 1953. The rank patch on the front of his arctic jacket indicates Field Marshal status (RM).

Life Colonel Commandant This unique honour was bestowed on Admiral of the Fleet the Earl Mountbatten of Burma, who held the position from 1965 to 1979, when he was murdered in Ireland. During the Second World War, Lord Mountbatten was head of Combined Operations and saw the first Royal Marines in Commando formations.

Colonels Commandant The Corps has four such officers, normally retired Royal Marines general officers, and they serve for four years. Colonels Commandant wear the uniform of a general officer but with the rank insignia of a colonel. This is another appointment in the gift of the Queen.

Honorary Colonel This appointment, made in 1981, is held by HRH Crown Prince Harald of Norway, the first member of a foreign Royal family to be so honoured.

SERVICE APPOINTMENTS

Commandant General Reporting to but not a member of the Admiralty Board, the Commandant General (CGRM) is an officer of Lieutenant General rank. He is responsible to the Vice Chief of the Naval Staff and normally occupies the position for three years. He is supported by his Chief of Staff (a Major General) and the Department of the CGRM located in the Main Building of the Ministry of Defence in London.

Guard duty at Windsor Castle in 1986 was the first opportunity for the Royal Marines to show off the SA80 rifle in public, and another chance to wear the ceremonial Blue uniform of which the Corps is so justly proud (RM).

Lieutenant-General

Major-General

Major General Royal Marines, Training Reserve and Special Forces is headquartered at Royal Marines Eastney, Portsmouth.
Major General, Commando Forces has operational control of the field force units of the 3 Cdo Bde remaining in the United Kingdom, if the Brigade has been deployed overseas.

INSIGNIA OF RANK

GENERAL OFFICERS

Lieutenant General The shoulder badge is a crown over crossed baton and sabre, with a cap badge of a gold crowned lion over a crown over crossed batons within a laurel wreath. The cap peak features two rows of embroidered gold oakleaf.

Major General The shoulder badge is a star, more generally known as a pip over a crossed baton and sabre; the beret badge is a lion over a crown over a crossed baton and sabre within a laurel wreath.

Brigadier This rank wears a shoulder badge of a crown over three pips in triangular formation with the point upwards. The beret badge is a crowned lion over a crown. A brigadier commands 3 Commando Brigade Royal Marines, the main field force.

FIELD OFFICERS

Colonel He wears a shoulder badge of a crown over two pips all in line; the beret badge is that of the brigadier. A full colonel is usually a senior staff officer.

Lieutenant Colonel The shoulder badge is a crown over a single pip and the beret or cap badge is the Corps badge. 'Half' colonels command the Commando units.

Brigadier

Colonel

Lieutenant-Colonel

Major

Major This rank is denoted by a crown worn on the shoulder; the cap and beret badges are the same. A major commands some of the specialist units, including the Cdo Bde Air Sqn.

Major (now Lieutenant Colonel) Richard Dixon RM is pictured wearing arctic combat kit for skiing, including the DPM cap which often replaces the green beret. For most operations in the snow, Royal Marines wear white overclothing to match the ski poles and straps shown in this picture (RM/3 Cdo Bde).

Captain

Lieutenant

2nd Lieutenant

Warrant Officer 1

JUNIOR OFFICERS
Captain The company commander is denoted by the three pips in a straight line on the shoulder, with the head–dress badges as for the major. Some of the specialist units are commanded by a captain.
Lieutenant As for the captain but only two pips are worn.
Second Lieutenant As for the captain, but only one pip is worn.

WARRANT OFFICERS
Warrant Officer 1/Regimental Sergeant Major The Royal Coat of Arms is worn on the lower sleeve.
Warrant Officer 2/Company Sergeant Major A crown within a laurel wreath is worn on the lower sleeve.

NON-COMMISSIONED OFFICERS
Colour Sergeant Three chevrons, point down, are worn on the upper arm with a crown over them.

Warrant Officer 2

Colour Sergeant

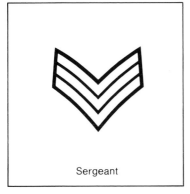

Sergeant

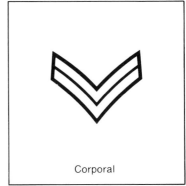

Corporal

Sergeant Three chevrons only.
Corporal Two chevrons are worn on the upper arm.
Marine No distinguishing insignia other than special skill badges (see page 143).

RANK EQUIVALENT TO OTHER SERVICES

Below the rank of full colonel, the Royal Marines and British Army officer ranks do not directly relate, except at sea, as the table below shows:

Royal Marines	Royal Navy	British Army	Royal Air Force
Lieutenant-Colonel	Captain	Colonel	Group Captain
Major	Commander	Lieutenant-Colonel	Wing-Commander
Captain	Lieutenant-Commander	Major	Squadron Leader
Lieutenant	Lieutenant	Captain	Flight Lieutenant

Royal Marines	Royal Navy	British Army	Royal Air Force
Acting Lieutenant	Sub Lieutenant	Lieutenant	Flying Officer
Second Lieutenant	Midshipman	Second Lieutenant	Pilot Officer
WO1/Regt Sgt Maj	WO	WO1/Regt Sgt Maj	None
WO2/Coy Sgt Maj	None	WO2/Coy Sgt Maj	WO
Colour Sgt	Chief Petty Officer	Staff Sergeant	Flight Sergeant
Sergeant	Petty Officer	Sergeant	Sergeant
Corporal	Leading Seaman	Corporal	Corporal
Lance Corporal	Able Seaman	Lance Corporal	Leading Aircraftman
Marine	Ordinary seaman	Private	Aircraftman

ROYAL MARINES BADGES

DRESS BADGES

Insignia Two shoulder flash designations are worn by the Royal Marines. Commando-trained officers and men have the flash 'Royal Marines Commando' in scarlet on a navy blue background and bandsmen have 'Royal Marines Band Service' in a similar fashion. The keen observer will also notice that there are 'Royal Navy Commando' shoulder flashes and these are restricted to the aviation, medical, dental, chaplain and certain support staffs who are attached to the Royal Marines for operations in Norway and other locations.

Colour Sergeants These senior non-commissioned officers have a distinctive insignia, wearing a gold-wire embroidered globe over

crossed Union Flags within a laurel and with a crown above. The badge is worn above the sergeant's chevrons in blue and lovat uniform.

Provost Sergeants These 'policemen' have inverted chevrons on the right cuff.

Specialist qualifications Most SQ badges are worn only on the lovat uniform tunic and their position on the sleeve depends on the wearer's level of qualification. First class holders have the qualification insignia above their chevrons, whereas second and third class holders wear them on the left cuff.

The three classes of SQ are important indicators of the wearer's abilities and prowess in a particular field. First class awards are indicated by a crown, second class by two pips, third class by one pip. Badges are gold on blue for blue uniform and green for lovat dress. The SQ is denoted by the initials for the skill, mounted over a double laurel branch curving upwards. Current SQs are:

Assault Engineer (AE): responsible for demolition, explosives, mine clearance and laying.

Air Gunner (AG): responsible for navigation and TOW anti-tank missile engagement. Badge is to Army Air Corps pattern, a 'G' with a single wing. This SQ may be discontinued as a result of the new helicopter crewing arrangement being introduced by the British Army.

Clerk (C): responsible for administrative and clerical duties.

Cook (K): responsible for food preparation and cooking in the field, aboard ship and in Royal Marines establishments.

Driver (D): responsible for the driving, care and maintenance of vehicles from motorbikes and Land Rovers to over-snow BV 202s and articulated lorries. Badge is a four-spoke wheel.

Heavy
Weapons

Drill & Platoon
Weapons

Drill Leader (DL): responsible for drill and parade ground instruction. Badge is crossed rifles.

Heavy Weapons (HW): responsible for the use and training of support company weapons, such as the 84mm Carl Gustav.

Landing Craft (LC): responsible for all small craft from landing craft utility to Rigid Raiders.

Mountain Leader (ML): responsible for cliff climbing, mountain climbing and forward reconnaissance duties as part of the Mountain & Arctic Warfare Cadre. Formally known as Cliff Leader (CL).

Physical Training (PT): responsible for the teaching and supervision of sport. Badge is crossed juggler's batons.

Platoon Weapons (PW): responsible for small arms and other military skills. Badge is crossed rifle, similar to Drill Leader (DL).

Signaller (S): responsible for the operation of radio and other signal/communications equipment. Badge is crossed flags.

Stores Accountant (SA): responsible for stores records and associated clerical work.

Swimmer Canoeist (SC): responsible for a host of waterborne roles, including that of the Special Boat Squadron.

Telecommunications Technicians (TT): responsible for the maintenance of radio and other signal/communications equipment. Badge is a ring with three lightning flashes each side.

Tradesman (T): are divided into a series of categories – armourer (personal weapons repair); artificer vehicle (supervision of major vehicle repairs); carpenter (all woodwork); illustrator (works in Unit Intelligence sections); metalsmith (vehicle repairs); printer (Corps and Royal Navy establishments); vehicle mechanic (servicing road vehicles). Badge is crossed hammer and pincer.

Not all SQs rate a separate badge and these include butcher (B), equipment repairer (ER), groom, light vehicle driver (LV) and radio operator (RO). Other badges include marksman's badge, parachute wings, pilot's wings (which follow the Army Air Corps pattern) and the sniper's badge. Recruit section leaders at CTCRM Lympstone wear a scarlet diamond on the left upper arm.

King's Badge This is awarded to the best all round recruit. The badge is a Royal cipher of GR (for King George V) over laurel branches and it is worn on left upper sleeve for the whole of the man's service, even when commissioned.

BAND BADGES

As the Royal Marines Band Service is a separate organization within

King's Badge

the Corps, it has developed its own badges, uniform and insignia. For example, the ceremonial No 1 blue uniform and white Wolseley-pattern helmet are worn. Junior musicians have a lyre collar badge instead of the Corps's globe and laurel, and buglers or drummers have the narrow scarlet trouser stripe rather than the broad stripe of other musicians. The helmet plate of the Band of CINCNAVHOME has the Royal ciphers of Queen Elizabeth II and King George V incorporated and the Band of HM Royal Marines Commandos wear a Prince of Wales plume.

In 1978, the Captain General, HRH The Prince Philip, directed that the year's best all-round musician or bugler would be awarded the Prince's Badge of a silver lyre, surmounted by a crown to be worn throughout his Royal Marines service.

Bugler (Bug): responsible for playing the bugle and the drums. Badge is a drum.

Musician (Musn): responsible for playing a range of musical instruments as part of the Royal Marines Band Service. Badge is a lyre.

Musician

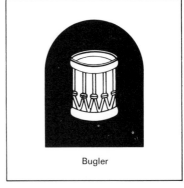

Bugler

A close-up of the SA80 self-loading rifle which is replacing the SLR as the personal weapon of the Royal Marine Commando. The weapon is lighter and smaller than its predecessor (RM).

COMBAT DRESS AND EQUIPMENT

Temperate combat dress is the most commonly-worn combat clothing and consists of a jacket and trousers in DPM (Disruptive Pattern Material). This is a material of olive green, black, brown and sand in colour, which has also become popular with non-military people for casual and working gear. The jacket has four patch pockets with buttoned flaps, buttoned cuffs and is fitted with draw-strings at the waist and around the bottom. At the front there is a full-length zipper and buttons, whilst some have a crutch flap and head-over cover.

Royal Marines are issued with a sleeveless quilted jerkin to go under the jacket, but this is uncomfortable and rarely worn. Many RM personnel supplement such clothing with privately purchased goods from such retailers as Survival Aids in Cumbria. This was brought to the attention of the media during and immediately after the Falklands conflict.

The long trousers can either be DMP pattern or lightweight olive green. The waist has loops for the webbing belt (in barracks, the traditional stable belt in Corps colours is worn). Various undergarments are worn depending on the location and role, but all are olive green or DMP.

Like the other services, the Royal Marines wear the drab, heavy, olive jersey and the rifle troops have been issued with the black leather combat gloves developed in Northern Ireland.

For arctic operations, the Corps has been issued with various thermal garments with the general proviso that multi-layered clothing is the best insulator against the cold, and it also allows the wearer

Below and overleaf *The modern battlefield is a dangerous place for a Royal Marine. Besides the more tradition threats of bomb and bullet is the nuclear, biological and chemical (NBC) weapon. To counter the threat, the UK Ministry of Defence and Remploy have developed special clothing, and illustrated here is that worn by 3 Cdo Bde Air Sqn and the Naval Air Commando support squadrons, which consists of the NBC Mk 1 aircrew coverall inner to protect against critical burns and all known chemical agents, the special hood, and the full olive drab protective suit which protects against all known biological and chemical agents. The marine is also wearing the Avon S10 respirator, gloves and boot covers; aircrew can wear the Negretti Aviation AR 5 respirator.*

to strip down when working – digging snow holes, emplacements or other features. A windproof, white-coloured smock and trousers are generally issued, together with special sheepskin mittens and ski–boots. Some units, including the Mountain & Arctic Warfare Cadre (see page 6) have Canadian-pattern Mukluk and snow shoes.

Although the green beret is *de rigueur* for Commando operations, the Royal Marines have been issued with the new British Army glass reinforced plastic combat helmet. The Corps has also been issued with a range of nuclear-biological-chemical (NBC) clothing made by Remploy. This is a paper-charcoal garment consisting of smock, trousers, overboots and gloves which lasts about three days before needing to be changed. The standard Avon S10 respirator is worn by ground-based marines, whilst aviators wear the Negretti AR 5.

SELECTION, RECRUITMENT AND TRAINING

The selection of men for the Royal Marines is thorough and demanding as befits one of the world's most professional and elite services. The Corps relies on good leaders at all levels of command where it is not just physical ability but also a high degree of common sense and intelligence that is required.

OFFICER SELECTION

Competition is high for direct entry to the RM Officers Course and the initial selection is in two parts: Potential Officers Course held at CTCRM Lympstone (Devon), and Admiralty Interview Board held at HMS *Sultan* (Gosport).

Potential Officers Course lasts for two days and consists of various tasks to give an indication of the candidates' physical fitness and mental aptitude for leadership. Besides the Tarzan and Assault courses, the spoken and written ability of the candidates is scrutinized. It is not just a matter of the RM looking at the candidate, but also there is an opportunity to talk with young officers under training. If the candidate passes the course, he is selected to attend the AIB.

Admiralty Interview Board examines the motivation, character, personality and general aptitude of candidates to become Royal Marines officers. It takes one-and-a-half days and includes a board in front of a selection panel chaired by an RM Colonel at the Admiralty Interview Board, for RN, RM and WRNS officers.

OFFICER TRAINING

Having been selected by the Ministry of Defence for training as a young officer, the candidate is given a probationary commission in the Royal Marines and begins two years of hard training at Lympstone (one year) and with a Commando as a rifle troop commander. It is said that only one in a hundred applicants successfully completes the second year. A new training system with greater emphasis on academic pursuits is due to start in 1989.

Royal Marine Commando selection for officers and other ranks is tough. The idea is to prepare the recruit for anything which he might face in a career as one of the world's most professional fighting men. At the Commando Training Centre, Lympstone, an instructor puts a party of recruits through part of the assault course (CTCRM).

Initial Officer Training takes place at Lympstone to give the candidate a general idea of military life, including drill, weapon handling and fitness. General service customs, background and responsibilities are taught.

Part 1 Military Training is the Commando test which tests the candidate's stamina and fitness to the limit. This training period includes battle fitness techniques, such as endurance and speed marches in full fighting order, before the five weeks of the Commando test at the end of which the coveted green beret is awarded. The Royal Marines stress that personal motivation is vital to success on the course, including the ability to complete the 30 mile (48 km) speed march in well under the optimum eight hours.

Academic tests and examinations are also carried out as the Corps is looking for an intelligent but tough leader in its future officer material. Current affairs, military law and administrative skills are also vital.

Part 2 Military Training lasts for the final 19 weeks of the course and is centred on the needs of the Royal Marines officer to know and understand the tactics involved in fighting as light infantry. Exercises are regularly carried out on Dartmoor and in Scotland. Tactics include attack and defence, section briefings, interpretation and dissemination of information, the use of support weapons, vehicles and various aircraft and the organization of troop movements.

Rifle Troop Command is the second phase of the young officer's training, which is really a matter of applying the training which has just been completed. Leading the 33 men of a rifle troop is demanding, especially when the troop sergeant could be an NCO of at least 12 years' experience, including the Falklands and winter Norway. It is stressed that it is a matter of teamwork.

The troop might be part of a Mountain & Arctic Warfare Commando, involved in NEC operations or internal security in Northern Ireland, such as exercises in northern Norway, the Baltic approaches or the jungles of Brunei. Equally it could be that the young officer has to take his men to Northern Ireland for the aid-to-the-Civil–Power role. Success in completing that second year will mean confirmation of the young officer's place in an elite Corps with the opportunity to go on to staff and specialist roles.

OFFICER SPECIALISTS

Following confirmation of officer status the Second Lieutenant advances to Lieutenant RM within a matter of months, usually for the full service commission officer, after an academic course at Britannia Royal Naval College, Dartmouth. This course broadens the officer's potential and general education.

Between the ages of 26 and 29, the Lieutenant RM would hope to be selected to attend Junior Division of the British Army staff college at Warminster. Additional courses and examinations follow, including a chance to attend the Royal Naval College, Greenwich, the British Army Staff College, Camberley, the Royal Air Force Staff College, Bracknell or a NATO/Commonwealth Staff College. Successful completion of the courses will mean a third pip and confirmation of promotion to Captain RM.

There are opportunities for specialization giving the Royal Marines officer more and diverse skills as well as extra qualifications, such as:

Troop Officer: includes commanding new recuits through CTCRM Lympstone where there are 12 troops under training at any one time.

Intelligence Officer: directly responsible to the CO for the collecting, collating and disseminating of information. Officers are trained in the analysis and interpretation of various types of information and data. Presentation of the evaluation is also vital.

Signals Officer: qualification follows a six months radio communications course at Lympstone and at the British Army School of Signals at Blandford. Signals Officers are trained to operate radio nets up to and including Brigade level.

Heavy Weapons Officer: although the Royal Marines have only infantry force weapons, the need to effectively use and train on the Milan anti-tank guided missile and the 81 mm Mortar is vital to the Commando groups.

Weapon Training Officer: this officer supervises the training of RM personnel in the use of small arms and controls the weapon ranges used by the Corps. Maintenance of weapons used on the range also comes under the control of this specialist officer.

Motor Transport Officer: drivers and vehicles used to transport the Corps are controlled by officers with this qualification. The job is especially important in Norway, where over-snow Volvo BV 202 and Land Rover vehicles are required to operate in freezing conditions. The MT Officer must ensure that they are effective and available to the Corps for any aspect of mobility required.

Training in unfamiliar terrain : Royal Marine Commandos from 40 Cdo RM en route to Exercise Saif Sareea in the Perisan Gulf, having stopped off in Cyprus. Such exercises are comparatively rare but regarded as vital for the worldwide role of the Corps (RM/ A1 Campbell).

Landing Craft Officer: an interesting specialization for the landing craft, raiding craft and water craft operated by the Royal Marines. An LC Officer is trained at RM Poole, where the coxswain's course for navigation and seamanship is completed.

Pilot Officer: certain RM officers are selected through the RAF Biggin Hill Officers and Aircrew Selection Board system for training as helicopter pilots, either for the light helicopter of 3 Cdo Bde Air Sqn RM or on exchange with the Royal Navy air commando squadrons flying the Sea King HC 4. Training is carried out at the Army Air Corps Centre, Middle Wallop and follows the same pattern as the AAC, the equipment being almost identical.

Mountain Leader: a tough course on Dartmoor and remote locations, including northern Norway, to train and carry out Mountain & Arctic Warfare courses and operations, which involves all aspects of mountaineering, route finding, climbing and survival in cold temperatures. Operations behind enemy lines would be part of the war role of an ML Officer.

Physical Training Officer: Royal Marines are very fit and keep that way through continuous training. Officers supervise physical training at RM bases and training establishments.

Special Boat Squadron Officer: very little is released about this Special Force's officers. Recruits are trained to be excellent swimmers, canoeists, divers, parachutists, reconnaissance experts, navigators and demolition specialists. Officers with this qualification must be very fit, have high stamina and be of above average intelligence.

MARINE SELECTION

The Royal Marines describe themselves as a special breed of fighting men, equally at home on land or sea or in the air. A Royal Marine will be expected to serve in mountain country, tropical jungle or in the snows of the Arctic Circle without a second thought, so clearly it requires a special type of fitness and intelligence to be a Royal Marine.

For general duties with the Royal Marines Commandos and sea service with the warships of the Royal Navy, a young man aged between 16 and 17½ years can enlist as a Junior Marine. Training is undertaken at the Commando Training Centre at Lympstone (Devon) on the basic Commando course, but a Junior Marine will not see operational service until he is 18 years old and classed as a Marine. The basic requirements for all forms of entry are the ability to complete the selection tests, an interview, medical examination and the famous (now infamous!) PRC or Potential Recruits Course.

For those aged 17½ to 28 years, the usual method of entry is as a Marine for General Duties and Technical Branch selection, with the same initial tests and the Basic Commando Course (BCC). For those who have selected a career as a cook or clerk in the Royal Marines, there is additional specialist training after the BCC.

The Royal Marines also recruit non-Commando specialists with a ceremonial role in peacetime but who, as was proved in the Falklands conflict, have an important battlefield role in wartime as stretcher-bearers and medical assistants.

Those aged between 16 and 17½ years who want to train to be musicians, for service with RM bands both afloat and ashore, are given full military orchestral and dance band training at the Royal Marines School of Music, Deal (Kent). To be accepted into this facet of the Corps, the entrant must have passed a selection test, interview, medical examination which includes dental and fitness checks, and a musical aptitude test.

From 17½ to his 28th birthday, a recruit to the Band Service can enlist as a Musician (Royal Marines), but he must be a fully-trained musician as well as passing the selection and the other tests as imposed on the potential Junior Musician. After selection, the Musician (RM) undertakes a short training period at the School of Music.

The third musical recruitment slot is that of Junior Bugler which is also open to those who pass the selection and other tests, and are aged between 16 and 17½ years. The Junior Bugler is trained at the Royal Marines School of Music as a Drummer and Bugler for land and sea service.

The usual service engagement for a Royal Marines recruit is nine years on a Long Service and Reserve Engagement. This involves a full service career until the Marine is 27 and then service in the Royal Fleet Reserve for the residue of 12 years from the time of entry.

The training at Lympstone is reckoned to be tough and it lasts for eight months during which time the recruit is turned into a Commando. The most important thing to have, say the instructors, is the ability to use your mind to overcome problems, both physical and mental. The Royal Marines Commando is not a super-fit, super-

During specialist training at RM Poole, a marine will learn about every aspect of small boat handling, including the manoeuvring of a landing craft into the dock of an LPD, in this case HMS Fearless.

intelligent 'superman', but a serviceman with special skills and normal fitness.

On arrival at Lympstone, the recruit is placed in a troop with a young officer, probably second tour, in command and he is supported by an experienced sergeant and at least two corporals. Training starts with the necessary but at times tedious art of looking after kit and equipment. The recruit is taught to shoot, drill and to wear the Queen's uniform.

Living rough starts as early as the second week of Recruit Training and involves night patrols and marches in the moorlands around Lympstone. Other training activity includes a section on amphibious warfare taught at Royal Marines Poole, including the use of landing craft and Rigid Raiders.

Commando training starts after the first leave block, some three months into the training, and by this time the recruit's troop will have been reduced by natural wastage and the tough selection pro-

Above *An officer (centre, directing the other craft) will need to be that much better than his men and be capable of firm, professional leadership in every aspect of the Royal Marines work, including leading a Raiding Squadron (RM).*

Below *The Royal Marine Commando of today is equipped with the latest weapons yet expected to act from his own personal resources. This clearance patrol on the side of Loch Erne shows Mnes Adams, Morris and Robinson wearing the latest pattern glass reinforced plastic helmet and carrying the Royal Ordnance 5.56 mm rifle with infantry night sight (RM).*

cess. Drill gives way to special skills, including close familiarization with the General Purpose Machine Gun, the SA 80 personal weapon and other guns. Mortars and the 84 mm Carl Gustav anti-tank rocket are also taught.

Royal Marines Commandos are expected to take cliff faces, marshes, moors and rivers in their stride – the course sergeants expect a recruit to make and use a rope bridge in less than five minutes. Fitness is measured in a man's ability to complete the six-mile endurance course in 80 minutes, carrying a Self-Loading Rifle and personal equipment, or by completing the 30-mile moorland march in eight hours. Finally, the would-be Commando must be able to satisfactorily complete the three-day Dartmoor Test. Only then can he wear the Green Beret.

Specializations for the trained Royal Marine Commando include: vehicle mechanic who repairs and maintains all RM vehicles; armourer who inspects and repairs all platoon weapons; telecom mechanic who inspects and repairs all radios; metalsmith who carries out vehicle bodywork repairs; carpenter who carries all woodwork requirements; illustrator who makes maps and models for intelligence; printer who undertakes all typesetting and printing work; driver who drives all vehicles from staff car to 10-tonner.

Other specializations include service with the Commando Brigade Air Squadron (which includes selection courses at RAF Biggin Hill and training with the Army Air Corps at Middle Wallop), the Special Boat Squadron and other units already described in this book. Marines and NCOs are often put forward for officer selection and training, sometimes including a repeat of the Commando course.

A patrol from 40 Cdo during exercise Saif Sareea in Oman during November 1986, the first Out of Area trial for the SA80 personal infantry weapon (RM/PO Phot Campbell).

In November 1987, the exercise scenario for 40 Cdo was Purple Warrior in northern Scotland. The personal equipment reflects the change in climate, but the personal weapon remains the same (RM/PO Phot Campbell).

INDEX

Page numbers in *italics* indicate photographs.